THE WELLNE[SS]

GUID[E]

Complete
Self-Care

25 TOOLS
FOR STRESS RELIEF

ANNA PEREIRA

Featuring:

Ingrid Auer, Jill Alman-Bernstein, Dr. Donna Blevins,
Ilene Dillon, Dr. Laura Ellick, Dr. Dolores Fazzino,
Linda Gillan, Melissa Jirovec, Elizabeth Kipp,
Rosemary Levesque, Debbra Lupien, Jenine "J9" Mayring,
Carolyn McGee, David D McLeod, Rev. Jennifer Moore,
Jim Phillips, Carole Park, Kim Marie Pauline,
Laura Sharon, Nancy Stevens, Janette Stuart,
Jennifer Wren Tolo, Dr. Toni Warner-McIntyre,
Jennifer Whitacre, Suzy Woo

"We invest our time, energy and money in so many people and places and things, now it's time to make an investment in your greatest asset, YOU. This book will take you through real life stories, real women (and men) who are courageous enough to tell their truths, and real solutions to help us all live our lives being a better version of ourselves.

Real stories. Real thoughts. Real solutions.

As women, our lives are all so different, yet many of our struggles are the same. When you read these stories, you see a piece of you in each one.

This book is a tremendous resource for self-improvement, where doctors, coaches and therapists share personal stories, practical strategies and everyday tools to help facilitate your transformation to physical and emotional well-being."

–Karina LeBlanc,
2 X Olympian, 2012 London Games Bronze Medalist,
5 X FIFA World Cup participant
and Head of Women's Football at CONCACAF.

"In the busy world we live in we often prioritize ourselves to the end of the list, or simply just forget about us. We are too busy caring for others and other things; our family, our friends, our colleagues. Just one more email, one more call, the house chores, the school run, our pets to care for, even our car which needs service. But what about us?

This wonderful book of incredible stories from extraordinary people brings home the reality that if we don't take care of ourselves, we will not be able to take care of others. This book is not only beautifully written and full of stark reminders, tips, tools, and exercises to help us become the best we can be, it's a guide for total wellbeing; the wellness of body, spirit and mind. It's a powerful reminder and practical guide that will never leave my side, with notes in the margin and folded down corners. This is not a book to read and put back on the shelf, it's one to own, share, and refer to often. For me it's the start of my journey to total wellbeing."

–Kate Cooper-Fay,
CEO CXY Limited, Customer/Employee Experience
and Consumer behavior Specialist, Lawyer and Chartered Director.
Member of the Professional Boards Forum
and Fellow of the Institute of Sales and Marketing Management.

Receive hundreds of dollars-worth of wellness gifts
by signing up for our newsletter at

www.TheWellnessUniverse.com

DEDICATION

To all of the brave souls who step up every day and serve the world with their wellness practice. To those who help the world transcend and transform to their highest and greatest good. To those who hold space to help just one person to make it through their day. To those whose legacy will be spoken of as "he/she made this a better world" by easing suffering, encouraging strength, teaching us to cope and guide us to healing, empowerment, love and peace; This book is dedicated to the servants of wellness, our WU World-Changers. You heed the calling. You choose to serve. Thank you.

To those seeking wellness, inspiration, and a better life. To those who have said "enough is enough, I deserve happiness." To those who are vulnerable and ready to heal the pain. To those who know there is a better life on the other side of wherever you are. To those who step up for themselves, their families, their loved ones, and their community to show up as their best selves. To the seekers of a better life experience. To those who know love and peace starts with you, this book is dedicated to you.

To my husband, my friends, my WU Team, and our amazing authors, without you, none of this could be possible.

DISCLAIMER:

This book offers health and nutritional information and is designed for educational purposes only. You should not rely on this information as a substitute for, nor does it replace professional medical advice, diagnosis, or treatment. If you have any concerns or questions about your health, you should always consult with a physician or other healthcare professional. Do not disregard, avoid, or delay obtaining medical or health-related advice from your healthcare professional because of something you may have read here. The use of any information provided in this book is solely at your own risk.

Developments in medical research may impact the health, fitness, and nutritional advice that appears here. No assurances can be given that the information contained in this book will always include the most relevant findings or developments with respect to the particular material.

Having said all that, know that the experts here have shared their tools, practices, and knowledge with you with a sincere and generous intent to assist you on your health and wellness journey. Please contact them with any questions you may have about the techniques or information they provided. They will be happy to assist you further!

ISBN Paperback: 978-1-954047-06-8
ISBN eBook: 978-1-954047-07-5

CONTENTS

INTRODUCTION

"The path to healing is not linear.

It is not defined by time or circumstance.

Healing comes through our ability to let go,

receive and allow."

Anna Pereira

We believe in a "mind-body-spirit" approach to wellbeing. The Wellness Universe was created to bring together people around the world who make the world a better place through their support of health, wellness, and wellbeing for mind, body, spirit, and planet.

Complete self-care cannot be achieved unless we nourish all of our parts. Within this guide, I want to share with you 25 of our top resources from The Wellness Universe to help you manage, reduce, and relieve stress.

Balanced mental wellbeing, I feel, is the foundation for a wonderful life experience. We are more resilient, positive, and empowered when we're calm, centered, and joy-filled.

Stress can come from tangible and intangible sources. Knowing what decisions to make and what feeds stress or diffuses it is essential to happiness.

This guide is chock full of tools and amazing coaches, doctors, and therapists, to help you through a stressful moment as well as practices to incorporate into your life to manage stress and be pro-active about your mental health.

This guide is especially near and dear to my heart as I suffer with occasional anxiety. My mindfulness practice along with putting these kinds of tools into action have helped me. This makes me a better person, wife, and leader.

I hope you find at least one golden nugget in this guide that changes your life. I hope you connect with these featured author-experts, WU World-Changers. They are here for you and your total wellbeing.

Love,

Anna

CHAPTER 1

FINDING CALM IN DAILY ROUTINE

A STEP BY STEP GUIDE

by Nancy Stevens, Life and Health Coach

MY STORY

"The secret of your future is hidden in your daily routine."

Mike Murdock

Slivers of soft daylight stirred me from sleep, my eyes slowly adjusting to the early morning light. I wake with a start as I'm jolted by loud mental chatter about what I've missed. In the covering of early morning light, I don't feel wrapped in restful calm. My racing thoughts immediately tell me I'm already behind. I'm not even out of bed yet.

I have orders to pack and ship. I am volunteering as a reader in Zach's class today at 11:00 am. I've got to send out emails to my room moms. How do I give the boys time to rest and have a snack as soon as they get home while making sure they are dressed and ready to leave for their soccer game? I don't have a clue what time we'll eat tonight. I can't wait for this day to end.

Before marriage and motherhood, I didn't usually feel behind at the start of each day. I recall intentionally hitting the snooze button and rolling out of bed with just enough time to get ready and out the door as my workday began.

Daily life stress took up space in my essence full time soon after the birth of our adorable fourth son Zach. As a busy boy-mom, constant noise, fights, and friends in and out were commonplace in our home.

Most of my workday week mornings began with a take-charge attitude as I marched into the day with all that was expected while saving space for the unexpected.

I always felt rushed and in a race to get things done exactly as needed in the timeframe required. I took pride in wearing my well-earned badge as a dependable mom who got it all done.

I operated from an action-packed, always-on agenda out of necessity in the early days, and over time, this was a well-worn mindless habit. Checking off our daily boxes had become the status quo for me. Taking a break to unwind during the day was not a habit.

Where was I in all of this? Somewhere close to the bottom. Why? I believed what I did was my role and job. This was my identity. I lived to please others by showing up.

To me, this was adulting. Sacrifice, hustle, and checking off my family's daily to-do boxes were mainstays. I was a serial multitasker. This was my role, and I was really good at it.

As a busy working mom with four active sons ranging from two years through 12 years, time didn't stand still for me. My inner critic sent out daily reminders. *You have work to do. Get it done. Everyone is counting on you today and tomorrow and the next day. Don't let our sons down by forgetting something. My husband expects me to pick up the pace and tie up loose business ends. My business needs me too.*

I operated my days in a state of unknown constant stress. Oddly enough, everything felt normal from my hurried, scattered vantage point because I didn't know otherwise.

I didn't know how I pushed myself wasn't sustainable nor healthy physically and emotionally. My busy adulting lifestyle was high stress. I was the stressed-out version of the beloved "Energizer Bunny."

SUBTLE STRESS SIGNS

Operating my days in a whirlwind of constant motion began to push back against me. Feelings of resentment and frustration slowly crept into my emotional landscape. *Why was I the first one up and working till I went to bed? I feel like all my work to keep our home running doesn't matter. I'm a one-person show more often than not. The more I do, the more I need to do. I didn't sign up for this much work.*

Of course, I kept these feelings to myself because I was conditioned that it was good to be in a constant state of motion. After all, this is what it meant to be a woman, wife, and mom.

My normal bouncy self was becoming easily defensive. I noticed my frustration fuse was short. I became easily irritated by doing everyday household chores like putting dishes away and end of the day clean up. This was new, an unwelcome visitor.

I was so busy handling, managing, and navigating everyone else's needs that I had become my lowest priority.

MISSING COMPONENT

Self-care was hit or miss at best and took place when I felt it was "okay after everything else was done," or I was spent.

Taking a moment of self-care to unwind and decompress felt out of place to this active, people-pleasing, get-it-done mom.

Typical pseudo-self-care involved indulging in sugary sweets covertly hidden, or wine to wind down my day, or reclined in front of the TV. Yes, these moments numbed things down while having the opposite effect by widening the gap between stress and calm that I didn't know was causing these negative feelings and reactions.

Deep down, I knew I needed to give myself a much-deserved break, but struggled with both guilt and actually finding time for myself. I didn't know where to start.

THE UNIVERSE INTERVENES

Looking back from my vantage point today, it's very interesting to me how the universe showed up to get me attuned and ready for my upcoming course correction.

The universe/God placed a potential move from Oregon to Tennessee front and center in our lives. My husband and I shared a conversation leading up to pulling up our beloved Oregon roots and leaving all we had known together as a couple.

What do you think about moving to Nashville so I can pursue producing? We can always move back if this doesn't work out. What will our families think about us moving so far away? We have so much here we really don't need to move. If we don't move, we'll never know what could've been.

Thankfully we pushed past our fears and embraced a dream of unknown potential.

Our move closed off immediate support from friends and family that helped and supported us. What little free time I did have evaporated overnight. Amidst an emotionally stressful move, a glimmer of support revealed itself. A brand new gym opened in our neighborhood, offering free daycare and classes to members as a perk. I went in, took a tour, and signed up on the spot! A break for me was on the way!

Life has a way of knowing where and when to intervene! It makes sense that my journey into "trying on" self-care began with taking action and doing! After all, I was an excellent multitasker!

I showed up excited for my first class, which happened to be yoga because it was a daycare match for my busy schedule. I knew very little about yoga other than it provided stretching. During a space of silence and stillness at the end of class, we were invited to lay on our mats in a process named Savasana, an active rest while reclined. My teacher's words melted my stress, "Come to lying on your back. Let your body simply rest and be. You're right where you need to be. Breathe." This blissful invitation and her loving touch gave birth to a tear-filled awakening. I had permission to simply be me in that quiet moment during Savasana while lying with softly closed eyes on my mat.

Suddenly I realized I was the one who mattered; I was enough. I had found my home, a place to tend to my feelings and needs. I had permission here to care for me. I felt a release of unknown tension. Inner calm replaced what I had unknowingly carried into class.

I wanted more of this experience! This began the winding road of intentional connection to inner balance. Here as a group fitness student, I slowly learned the sneaky ways stress slips into life and how to release myself from its unfriendly icy grip eventually.

This deep shift opened the door to taking more classes growing more connected to myself, and pursuing instructor teacher training as a yoga teacher. I thought I was "doing" this once again for others. What the teacher training gave me was the beginning of my journey back to me.

Through yoga, I also began the practice of learning how to be present and mindful. Initially, this was quite a challenge, as it directly countered how I've always lived, a serial multitasker.

Learning mindfulness cultivated fertile soil that planted seeds for my personal growth and development as me, aside from my self given roles, titles, and duties.

I began to learn that life was not just a string of random happenings and reactions, but a beautiful complex fabric of emotional application, self-discovery, self-compassion, and releasing taking place every day. My journey was not a one-and-done but a winding road with beautiful twists and turns.

I learned that stress release is not in doing but in being; living congruently. Inner life creates a meaningful outer life. This is how I found myself. When I gave myself permission to do the work of finding myself, my outer and inner lives became one. Daily stress eased away, directed now from my calm inner self!

I figured out that not only did I have to create new inner life for myself, but I also had to create a routine of it to ensure I was nourished first. My daily morning routine of self-care helped me transform the stress into a life I love living that gives me peace and joy.

Through my yoga teacher, life coach, and mindfulness training, I learned that my personal daily routine was the ticket to an amazing life.

I can't wait to teach you how to create your own personal self-care routine, one of the keys to stress relief and a happier you.

YOUR BEST DAY IS THOUGHTFULLY CREATED BY YOUR INNER VOICE SPEAKING ON YOUR BEHALF. SHOW UP AND SHINE!

THE TOOL

A Step By Step Guide

The simple routine I'm sharing with you is intentional and personal. Think of your routine as the gas needed to power your car. Your routine equals gas that melts stress away by creating calm and focus.

For me, creating and following my morning routine changed my life from feeling untethered to grounded, calm, and connected. It set the pace and tone for my entire day. My morning routine completes and compliments me.

WHAT IS AN A.M. ROUTINE?

Your "A.M." routine is a set of intentional, personalized actions you do at the start of the morning before your day takes off with commitments and obligations like work outside the home or at home.

WHY CREATE A ROUTINE?

A routine provides structure, sequence, and flow to your daily life. Cultivating a personal daily routine places you in the driver's seat. With a personal routine, you control the flow and pace of how you wish your day to start, and this keeps the stress away while promoting calm and peace within you.

CALMING NOTE

Setting and implementing your personal routine isn't a one-and-done. As you move into this, it's important to notice what's working and what isn't. What feels life-affirming and what feels energy draining. Give yourself time to get used to your new routine for a while. Revise your routine once you know what is and isn't aligned with your needs. You'll know your routine is just right when upon completion each morning, you feel connected, cared for, and ready to go!

Four key elements to include in your routine.

- Body
- Mind
- Daily To Do's
- Materials for the day

BODY

Physical actions meant to lovingly prep my body at the start of the day.

MIND

Mental and emotional processes tending to my emotional center, mental state, and brain health!

DAILY TO DO'S

A listing of all key appointments and work/life items needing to be addressed and handled today. Most important to least.

MATERIALS FOR THE DAY

What physical items do I need on hand and ready to go today for work and personal use?

CHOOSE AND ASSIGN YOUR ACTION(S) TO EACH ELEMENT

BODY

Hydrate with a full glass of water.

Activate your body with some gentle total body stretching.

Coffee/Tea/Juicing if you take in a morning beverage.

Get moving (options) walking, biking, full out run, early morning fitness class, online workout, weight training, yoga workout. Do this as little as ten minutes up to a full workout.

Personal Hygiene: Shower, wash face, brush teeth, hair, makeup

Fuel: Food for later, breakfast if a breakfast eater.

MIND

GRATITUDE PRACTICE

Think, speak, or journal what brings in gratitude as these bubble up within you.

SILENCE AND STILLNESS PRACTICE/ MEDITATION/PRAYER

(Option 1) Sitting in silence and stillness: Find a quiet, distraction-free place to be still/silent. Try a five minute moment or longer.

(Option 2) Listening to a guided meditation from a smart device app.

(Option 3) Walking silence moving meditation 10-20 minutes using nature to nurture and reset.

AFFIRMATION PRACTICE

Recite internally or aloud a loving energizing statement.

Examples: I love myself. My self-love is a blessing. Everything is working for me as it's meant to. I am resilient and radiate. I'm solutions focused on the best outcome. I trust myself and my instincts. I am lovingly strong and impact others with this gift. I am a badass.

DAILY TO-DO LIST

Write out your six most important tasks (MIT's) you need to complete today based on urgency, job requirements, caregiving, household, community, etc.

ITEMS NEEDED FOR THE DAY

What specific items do you need to use and have on hand? (I now carry my notebook and pen and personal growth books in the car, so when I have downtime, I've got something to work on versus surfing social media on my phone.

Examples:

Clothes/shoes/accessories

Food and Water Bottle/Medicines/

Phone/Phone charger/Car keys

Hygiene items

Laptop/I-Pad/Backpack

CREATE A SIMPLE AND ACTIONABLE ROUTINE AT A PACE THAT ANSWERS TO YOUR SOULFUL SELF

Example: This is my actual daily AM Routine

5:30-6 am (Day Begins) wake up and get up.

6:10 am (Body) Hydrate with a full glass of water immediately after waking and after bathroom!

6:12 am (Body) Get my coffee started.

6:15 am (Body) Wash my face and apply my skincare products. I typically shower before bed. If not, I'll use this time to shower and add in time to dry/style my hair.

6:20 am (Body) Get dressed in work or workout clothes.

6:25 am (Body) Full body gentle stretch with full breaths (3-5 minutes) to awaken my muscles and tissues from sleep mode

6:30 am (Body/Mind) Walk outdoors 15-20 minutes with Doug, the dog. I practice gratitude and connect to God while walking. Nature is my spiritual zone and a must-do for full entry into the day yet to unfold.

6:30 am (Mind) While on my short morning walk with Doug: gratitude practice in silence. Prayer of thanksgiving offered up.

6:50 am (Mind) Once home from walking, seated meditation in my special room in our home 5 -10 minutes.

7:00 am (Mind) Affirmations and personal power statement, spoken quietly with confidence.

7:05 am (Body) Eat light breakfast.

If school is in session - help my teen son with breakfast and any request he has for his day.

7:15 am (Daily to-do list)

Using my notebook or planner, I sit and write out my most important tasks: MITs, to ensure I'm on top of appointments, client meetings, calls, errands, etc.

7:25 am (Items needed for the day) Gather my materials for the day:

In the morning, I teach classes. I keep my ready-packed fitness bag in the car.

Items needed daily:

Yoga mat

Filled water bottle

Energy bar/banana

Instructor gym bag

Lavender spritzer spray

7:35 am (Ready to go) Leave the house 25 minutes before 8:00 am class time. Balanced and energetically ready for the day at hand!

My routine is straight forward and simple, with each element following the next. As you create and move into your routine, you'll know how this feels and whether you'll revise and edit.

To get started, use this format:

1. Designate a specific element from the four key elements.
2. Assign an action to the element.
3. Choose a specific time.

EAT your routine!

- E. Element (body)
- A. Assigned action (hydrate)
- T. Time assigned to the action (6:15 am)

START SMALL AND KEEP IT SIMPLE. THIS IS YOU LOVING YOURSELF!

PUTTING IT ALL TOGETHER!

Always include your wake up time as part of your am routine. This places the energy of timeliness and accountability at the start of what you've chosen will follow.

7:00 Wake up and move from bed to begin my day.

7:05 (Element Body) (Assigned action) hydrate.

7:10 (Element Body) (Assigned action) gentle stretching.

7:20 (Element Mind) (Assigned action) gratitude practice.

7:25 (Element Body) (Assigned action) get dressed and ready for the day.

Start with a few pieces similar to those above but personalized according to your wants and needs. This is a calming routine and a beautiful beginning.

That's all there is to this. Here is to your balanced morning routine!

Nancy Stevens is an International Certified Coach, a #1 bestselling Amazon author of *The Beauty of Authenticity*, a lifestyle blogger with The Wellness Universe, a talk show host on News For The Soul.com radio, as well as co-hosting Soul Empowerment on The Wellness Universe's Learn It Live platform. She shares her passion for both shows on how to live impact-fully by intentional personal growth. She is an accomplished speaker, educating groups and organizations about personal development and healthy wellbeing. Nancy's calling is to connect and empower busy women to find and own calm, confidence, and happiness in all of their life so that they can be change-makers and positively impact others. When she's not working, Nancy loves spending time with her husband, a five-time Grammy Award winner, and their four young adult sons. https://www.thewellnessuniverse.com/world-changers/nancystevens/

CHAPTER 2

GRATITUDE

THE MAGICAL ELIXIR TO REDUCE STRESS, WORRY, AND ANXIETY

by Janette Stuart

MY STORY

That hot summer day in August 2019, I met with the nurse practitioner for my first post-surgical appointment following my Whipple procedure for pancreatic cancer. After a few pleasantries, she asked, "Are you ready to begin chemo next week?" I replied, "No, I was hoping I wouldn't need any additional chemo." I was thinking, *Heck, no, I don't want more chemo. I'm finally starting to get my strength back, taking only one nap per day, and after all this good news from my surgery and marvelous lab results, they want me to go back to chemo and feeling crappy again? No, thanks!* It didn't make sense to me or feel right that I'd need additional chemo with the results I had.

I had just had the major surgery a few weeks before. My surgical team removed the head of my pancreas, most of the duodenum (a part of the small intestine), a portion of the bile duct, and gallbladder, and I remained in the hospital for two weeks. I was blessed even to have the surgery because my case was borderline due to the tumor location and vein involvement.

I had excellent results from the surgery, clear margins, no lymph nodes were affected, my stomach was not compromised, and they felt they had removed the tumor in its entirety. My lab results showed that my cancer marker was now in the normal range. Yay! I received my miracle. I was so grateful.

My oncologist was out of the country for an additional three weeks, and the nurse practitioner consulted with a partner who recommended completing the next four rounds of chemo. That suggestion didn't feel right to me, and she told me as the patient, it was my right to decline their recommendation, and that no one could make me move forward with chemo or any treatment for that matter.

I decided to wait until my oncologist returned to get his opinion. I had expressed my feelings to my husband, sister, parents, and some dear friends about declining additional chemo until consulting with my oncologist. They all agreed with my sentiments given that chemo had been rough on me and that my prognosis following the surgery was so good. The chemo is named 5-fluorouracil, referred to as 5FU (aptly nicknamed I must say), and it's so fun to say, "FU, FU, FU, FU, and FU." One of my chemo nurses and I had a good laugh about this during one session.

I was beginning to feel good again around this time. I was healing from the surgery, eating well (although toddler-sized portions), and it had been almost four months since my last round of chemo. My hair was starting to come back, and the side effects of chemo were diminishing. During the months of biweekly treatments, I would have about two days where I would feel decent, and the rest of the days, I felt weak, lethargic, blah, and nothing tasted right.

I began to regain a taste for my favorite drink: water, and the cold sensitivity was lessening. From the beginning of chemo in February 2019, the sensitivity to cold was extreme. Holding room temperature silverware was painful. Turning on metal faucets to wash my hands was torture. Even room temperature fluids would cause shooting pain from my mouth to the top of my head, and forget about anything cold. I wore white cotton gloves to help the matter. I was weary of not feeling well for so many months.

I had prayed extensively about the next right steps for my treatment. I didn't want my preference for no additional chemo to cloud my judgment or interfere with my long-term prognosis. I surrendered the decision to divine timing and order.

My parents and I were in the tiny examination room that afternoon last September, feeling nervous while waiting for our turn. It was a hot day, and the air-conditioner was humming along great, keeping us cool. I was holding my intention in my rapidly beating heart. My oncologist walked into the room that afternoon and quickly stated: "I recommend no further treatment at this time since there is no evidence of disease." *Yippee, amen, and hallelujah!* I jumped down off the examination table and asked if I could hug him. He said yes, and all four of us shared hugs and immense gratitude. I thanked him for his excellent care, and he brushed it off and said, "All I did was administer the poison."

I felt like I was walking on cloud nine as we walked to the car. I was so, so grateful for this fantastic news. It was almost more than I could bear. I felt taller, lighter, and freer than I had in months. It was yet another example of the miraculous developments upon my healing journey.

I was and still am so thankful for the many people who loved and supported me along my healing journey. Friends, family, and even strangers were praying for my family and me. People showered us with love, care, physical and spiritual gifts to lighten our burdens, and I am eternally grateful.

THE TOOL

GRATITUDE

What is gratitude? It generally stands for the quality or feeling of being grateful, thankful, or appreciative. It is a high vibration feeling.

Gratitude is the magical elixir to reduce stress, worry, and anxiety. There is actual science behind the concept and practice of gratitude, which I'll share below; it's not just "woo-woo."

Gratitude is a "natural antidepressant," created through the production of the feel-good hormones dopamine and serotonin in our brain that improves our mood.

In the white paper from Ph.D.'s Russell and Fosha in 2008, *"Transformational Affects and Core State in AEDP: The Emergence and Consolidation of Joy, Hope, Gratitude, and Confidence in (the Solid Goodness) of the Self,"* they explain the neuroscience behind the concept of gratitude as three areas of benefit: psychological, physical, and social.

Psychological Benefits (A Happier You)

- Positive emotions and thoughts

- More aware and awake

- Increased self-satisfaction

- Enhanced mood

Physical Benefits (A Fitter You)

- Strong immune system

- Fewer body aches and pains

- Optimum blood pressure and cardiac function

- Better sleep-wake cycles

Social Benefits (A Better You)

- Better communication

- More empathy

- Stronger interpersonal relationships

- More likability among group members

- More involvement as a team member

From an early age, we are taught to express gratitude as a courtesy to others for what they do or give to us. We're taught to say "please" and "thank you." We're encouraged to write thank-you notes, draw a picture, or take a picture with the gift to express our gratitude. Perhaps once a year at Thanksgiving, or after a special event, we are encouraged to express appreciation to others for our material possessions.

We may have been taught to say a blessing for our food or to say "grace." The word grace comes from the same Latin root word "grata or gratia" as gratitude and means expression for a gift (generally meaning food) freely given and unearned.

As science shows, gratitude is good for us in a multitude of ways. If gratitude is so good for us, why don't we express it more frequently?

Generally, we have not been taught to express gratitude regularly or to incorporate the benefits of it into our daily lives. We may have heard the term of counting our blessings, but how do we do that? We'll learn more about the practice of gratitude below.

The invitation in this chapter is to find a way to incorporate gratitude more regularly into your life. There are several ideas listed, and gratitude is beneficial for you, your family, friends, coworkers, neighbors, and the world. Our gratitude creates a massive ripple of love and appreciation out into the world. Think of gratitude as a sacred self-care magical elixir or potion.

"Being grateful all the time isn't easy. But it's when you least feel thankful that you are most in need of what gratitude can give you: perspective. Gratitude can transform any situation. It alters your vibration, moving you from negative energy to positive. It's the quickest, easiest, most powerful way to effect change in your life — this I know for sure."

Oprah Winfrey

Gratitude raises your vibration level, and when you are in a state of gratitude, it is impossible to feel stress, worry, or anxiety. I like to envision myself "swimming in a sea of love and gratitude," actually surrounding myself in it, being one with gratitude, breathing it, exuding it as if living my life like a prayer of thanksgiving. That is my vision. Do I always attain it? No, not hardly, and yet it is my intention and goal.

Ways to use gratitude as a magical elixir to reduce stress, worry, and anxiety.

1. Gratitude List or Journal – This is a way to list or "count your blessings." Ask yourself what you are currently grateful for and why you are thankful for each thing. Think or write those things down. Some folks list 3-5 things each day upon waking or before retiring for the night. You can keep the list on your phone, in a notebook, journal, tablet, or hold it in your heart.

2. Gratitude Jar – This is another way to gather your gratitude or "count your blessings" positively and in a tangible way. Start by writing your gratitude(s) on a slip of paper, add the date, and list why you are grateful for them. Fold it up, and place it in a glass jar you have labeled or decorated to collect your blessings. I used to keep my gratitude jar on my dining table and would add my slips of paper on a pretty regular basis and found I needed a bigger jar before the end of the year. Hold a private year-end ceremony or ritual to review these blessings and relive the wonder and goodness you have experienced.

3. Gratitude Meditation – Quieting our hearts and minds to allow a sense of gratitude and thanksgiving to flow is another way to reduce stress, worry, or anxiety. There are many free meditations online and apps with lots of possibilities for calm at our fingertips.

4. Gratitude Walk – This is a daily ritual for me as I walk my dog. I am on the lookout for beauty in our midst and cultivating a sense of peace and gratitude. Moving your body in nature (even in your own neighborhood) is a wonderful practice.

5. Gratitude Hands – This is a fun project for family get-togethers, especially if there are young children. Trace the little one's handprint on construction paper, cut out, and write their name and date on the back. You can add gratitude about the child, the event, or family on the fingers if you'd like. You can frame them, place them in a scrapbook, family bible, or photo collection or collage. It is a timeless treasure. You can make many of them and give them to friends, grandparents, or relatives as a priceless memento.

6. Leaves of Gratitude Collage – This is similar to the Gratitude Hands project mentioned above. You can create leaf-shaped pieces of construction paper in various fall colors, and at your family Thanksgiving dinner, ask each person to write something they are grateful for. Collect those leaves and create a holiday collage you can decorate your home with for the holidays. This activity is another timeless treasure.

7. Daily Group Gratitude – You can join with some friends or family members to share your daily gratitude via email or on a social media platform. You may want to join Angel Angles Angel Circle of Gratitude group on Facebook to cultivate gratitude further and reduce stress, worry, and anxiety. You can also share your daily gratitude with friends or family around the dinner table.

8. Gratitude Projects – I just celebrated my 60th birthday this year. To honor the gift of my life and the gratitude I felt, especially after surviving pancreatic cancer, I chose to write 60 thank you letters to friends and family members special in my life. I hand-wrote each letter and customized it to the individual. Writing thank you notes is a sure-fire way to cultivate more gratitude in your life and reduce stress, worry, and anxiety.

9. Gratitude Videos – There are thousands of gratitude videos that can boost your mood and perhaps motivate you to create your own version of the topic. I recently watched 365 Days of Thank You (TedExYouth – San Diego video presentation) by Brian Doyle and loved it. This young man had a life-altering experience and wanted people to know how important they were in his life and chose to express gratitude to a different person each day for a year. WOW, powerful.

10. Gratitude Affirmations – Affirmations are short, positive, powerful tools to shift our vibration. Here are several affirmations about gratitude that you may want to incorporate in your daily quiet time or routine.

   • There is always something to be grateful for.
   • I begin my day thinking of three things I am grateful for.
   • I end my day thinking of three things I am grateful for knowing it helps sow the seeds for a good night's rest and a better day ahead.

- I am grateful for the gift of my life and my vibrant health.
- I am grateful for the gift of friends and family in my life.
- I am grateful for the many freedoms I experience in my life.
- I am grateful for my home, my job, and the many tools that bring ease into my life.
- I radiate gratitude for all my many blessings.
- I am so grateful for the beauty and wonder of nature in my midst.

11. Gratitude Intentions – Intentions are ways of choosing or focusing upon a result or outcome. Below are several intentions you may want to incorporate into your daily quiet time or routine.

- Today, I choose to cultivate more joy and delight in my life, using gratitude.
- Today, I notice the ordinary gifts in my life.
- I choose to radiate a sense of appreciation throughout my day.
- I allow my sense of childlike wonder to shine forth.
- I escape to nature to cultivate a more profound sense of well-being.
- I count my blessings regularly throughout the day.
- Today, I am on the lookout for miracles and synchronicity.
- I release stress, worry, and anxiety when I focus on gratitude.

The more gratitude you cultivate in your life, the less stress, worry, and anxiety you will have. According to the Law of Attraction, the more you focus on something, the more of it you receive. If you want more gratitude, focus on cultivating more gratitude in your life. The ideas listed are some of the many ways you can enjoy the self-care and grow more appreciation in your life starting today as you send ripples of love and gratitude out to benefit the world.

Thank you for being on this journey with me and creating a wave of positivity for the world. Visit my link below in the bio for more gratitude goodies, including an audio recording of me reading this chapter.

Janette Stuart: Emissary of Joy at Angel Angles and Well-Being and Wonder is a beacon of love, joy, peace, and gentleness. She's a #1 Best Selling author, blogger, military mom, and pancreatic cancer survivor who uses the gift of her words and positivity to assist others to embrace their divinity using tools such as her series of devotionals called "On a Path of Joy."

As an angelic practitioner, she shares goodness and grace and the healing beauty of nature frequently to inspire others, including 1:1 angel sessions. She has developed an inspirational card deck called "Love Notes from The Divine" and is co-creator of "Words of Wisdom Guidance Cards" and shares daily messages of love and encouragement on social media.

Janette lives in the San Francisco Bay Area with her husband Mark, and their boxer dog Spike. She has a grown son proudly serving in the United States Coast Guard and is one of her biggest joys in life. Janette loves cooking, being out in nature, writing, and has an impressive collection of stationery, pens, and journals.

Connect with her https://www.thewellnessuniverse.com/world-changers/janettestuart/ and meet her at SoulTreat 2021 in Boone, NC.

CHAPTER 3

TAPPING FOR TURBULENT TIMES

RELEASE EMPATHIC DISTRESS WITH EMOTIONAL FREEDOM TECHNIQUES

by Rev. Jennifer Moore, Accredited EFT Master Trainer

MY STORY

Beneath the perfume of my hydrangea and purple butterfly bushes, a mixture of wet grass and horse manure wafts over from our neighbor's pasture. I unscrew the lid of my blue mason jar and sip well water I'd grabbed from the fridge. The taste of wild rose elixir I'd added a few jarfuls earlier still adheres to the glass. The warmth of the afternoon sun balances the cool breeze blowing across my skin. I close my eyes. I imagine I'm at the beach. The rustle of branches becomes ocean surf. I open my eyes. I watch black poplar and white pine sway and flicker in the golden light we Mainers only see in September. It's a perfect late summer, 72-degree day. All is well in my world. Friends, family and clients are fine. I'm safe. I'm healthy. I have a roof over my head and food on my shelves. So why am I feeling so off?

Why does this seemingly glorious day feel so unbearable? Is there a disturbance in the field? Am I sensing imminent danger? Do I need to brace for yet another disaster? Did one of the new (and supposedly calming) herbal supplements trigger an adverse reaction? Did I eat food that threw my system off? Did I reactivate some old emotional wound? Am I finally just losing it?

Logically, my funk just doesn't make sense.

RECOGNIZING EMPATHIC DISTRESS

For most of my teen years and early adulthood, this uneasiness was my regular state. Feeling calm and focused was the exception, not the rule for me. I was what some people call a high-strung, emotional hot mess. Tools such as journaling, breathwork, prayers, flower essences, bodywork, and movement helped but rarely provided lasting relief. Affirmations only amplified the contrast between my desires and my reality. I knew I was highly sensitive and intuitive. I knew I absorbed the thoughts, feelings, energy, and sensations from the world around me. I just didn't get how deeply my empathic nature affected me.

Occasionally I'd tell a loved one how stressed and overwhelmed I felt. My confessions were usually met with indifference or outright invalidation. "You're overreacting. You're taking this too personally. You're making a big deal over nothing. Just let it go. You aren't some starving kid living in a war-torn country. Get over it." I could only conclude the problem was me. This led to years of antidepressants, self-medicating with cigarettes, pounds of M&Ms, greasy take-out, and distracting myself with one romantic impossibility after another.

ACCEPTING SUPPORT

It took being in enough pain to get "sick and tired of being sick and tired," and admit I needed help. I'll be forever grateful to my first good therapist. I'd tried seeing others, but psychotherapy didn't work until I found someone as psychic as me. She showed me that a lot of the baggage I struggled with wasn't actually mine. Ironically, being willing to examine my own stuff allowed me to recognize just how much distress I'd taken on from others. This was the beginning of my transformation from psychic sponge to thriving empath. First, I learned to acknowledge and express what I felt; then I learned to distinguish my issues from external pain and suffering.

However, being able to recognize what was mine and what wasn't didn't address the stuff I already carried. Not only did I need to differentiate my distress from others', but I also needed to find an effective way to release it.

SEEKING RELIEF

Over the next two decades, I experimented with many healing modalities, yet I still woke up most days churning with anxiety. Like so many people I've worked with over the years, I underestimated how profoundly my sensitivity impacted my well being. I'd been taught to divert my attention from anything negative and focus on the positive. I'd learned to visualize a ball of light around me and to send love and forgiveness to who or whatever had gotten my goat. Trying to control my empathic nature worked about as well as ordering a toddler to stop having a tantrum. Self-medicating, denial, and suppression of my abilities brought temporary relief, but none of them worked very long. Much to my chagrin, I discovered that try as I might to ignore negativity, it still festered beneath the surface until I couldn't deny it anymore. So much of my anxiety and despair came from picking up the pain, suffering, and struggles of the world around me. I wanted to make a difference and help our planet, but my unresolved empathic overwhelm just added to the mess.

Fifty years ago, most people could compartmentalize their feelings. They could hide their struggles. Not anymore. Even if someone tries to suppress feelings of rage, terror, or grief, others can sense trouble under the surface. Today we're engaged in an ever-expanding feedback loop. More people are picking up global pain and struggling with it. Left unattended, it ripples back into the world. This is why I believe it's crucial to learn not only to recognize what we're thinking and feeling but also how to shift it. We empaths, lightworkers, creatives, and other sensitives must address our inner turmoil to prevent broadcasting it to the outer world. To be part of the solution, we must learn how to heal and release our empathic distress. That's why I'm sharing EFT (Emotional Freedom Techniques) with you. With more than three decades of personal and professional healing work under my belt, I've never found anything more versatile or effective. One of the best things about it is that you can "try this at home!"

DISCOVERING EFT

Also known as Tapping, EFT is like emotional acupuncture. It balances the body's energy system and reboots the amygdala: the part of our brain that governs our fight or flight response. Tapping works with the meridians in our body to calm thoughts and feelings and promote relaxation. It allows us to think more clearly and to release negative emotions and limiting beliefs. You focus on a challenge, then gently tap or apply light pressure with your fingertips to acupuncture points on the head, face, torso, and hands.

Now, I won't lie, even though I'm pretty woo, the first EFT demo I watched seemed kinda weird. Some guy repeating, "I deeply and completely love and accept myself," while he tapped on the side of his hand looked downright cheesy to me. However, I was struggling enough to experiment. For a few years, I'd tap sporadically. I'd try it on random things. But, truth be told, I was barely going through the motions. As you might imagine, my half-hearted efforts yielded half-assed results. Then, in a moment of desperation, I discovered what EFT could actually do.

For nearly three decades, I'd struggled with anxiety and PTSD following a car accident. My worst trigger was treacherous road conditions. Sitting in the passenger seat while driving north during an ice storm was terrifying. Despite freezing rain and a slush-covered highway, I shifted from panic to calm after only a few rounds of tapping. I experienced true relief for the first time in my life, and I was hooked.

You might wonder, *what changed? What made this time different?* When I'd tried tapping before, I used it for vague issues. This time my distress was intense and identifiable. When I started tapping on my fear of the icy road, I knew exactly what I was dealing with. I could feel tension in my solar plexus and envision impending doom. I was tapping on something specific. There's a significant difference between following generic tap-along scripts or videos from the internet vs. targeting issues precisely. This first approach yields mediocre results, whereas I've witnessed countless miracles with the second.

I'm going to teach you how to work with a physical sensation to access what's going on and then shift it. The reason I start with the body is because it inevitably leads to everything else. One of the biggest challenges empathic people face is feeling disconnected from their own bodies, thereby losing the distinction between themselves and the outside world. It doesn't matter if something started with you, or you picked it up elsewhere, the process is the same. Regardless of the source (or sources), tapping calms intensity. Focusing on your body helps you to find your baseline.

Before I go into detailed instructions, I want to answer the question that often arises for people new to EFT: "If I focus on my problems, won't it just make them worse?" Here's my response: there's a fine line between positive thinking and resistance. Perhaps you've heard the saying "what we resist, persists." Whether you continue to give it attention or not, the distress you've noticed is already there.

The greatest paradox in life is that acceptance is the key to untangling even the worst knots. EFT allows you to gently acknowledge your problem and transform it without getting sucked into the drama. Just as physical wounds must be cleaned before we bandage them, mental and emotional wounds need to be cleansed as well. There's a big difference between tending a wound and ripping open a scab. Please don't make a beeline to the worst event in your life and tap on every gory detail. That's the kind of stuff you bring to an accredited EFT practitioner. I suggest the opposite: stay in the shallow end of the pool. Start with simpler low-intensity issues. Tapping on what may seem small will bring relief to larger challenges as well.

THE TOOL

EMOTIONAL FREEDOM TECHNIQUES

In its simplest form, EFT breaks down into three repeating parts. It's called the Basic Recipe.

1. Identify and Rate
2. Acknowledge and Accept
3. Tap and Notice

This formula works whether you're dealing with physical sensations, challenging emotions, difficult past events, limiting beliefs, or any other kind of distress. Unless a clear emotion or internal message is readily apparent, I usually start with the body. It's been said: "EFT is simple. Humans are complicated." If you're like me, you know how to complicate everything. Empathic overwhelm often starts as a tangle. Being specific is the most efficient way to alleviate stress. Tapping on everything but the kitchen sink can temporarily take down the intensity, but precise EFT is a better way to shift the root cause. My dear mentor and master trainer of trainers, Jade Barbee, distinguishes the difference between general tapping and precise EFT as broadly tapping on something a mile wide and an inch deep or narrowly focusing on an issue that's an inch wide and a mile deep.

IDENTIFY AND RATE

EFT starts by noticing your thoughts, feelings, and sensations. Take a deep breath, tune into your body. Pay attention to anything that comes up. Use the following questions for further clarification.

- Am I experiencing something physical, mental, or emotional right now?
- How is this manifesting in my body?
- Am I experiencing any pain or unusual sensations?
- Exactly where in my body is it?
- How am I reacting or responding to this?
- If it had a color, what would it be?
- If it had an emotion, what would it be?

These answers provide what you'll tap on. For example, I feel a dull ache in my right shoulder joint. I don't like it. I notice it's triggering worry and concern. I close my eyes and imagine it's murky orange with flecks of bile green. I distill these details into my reminder: "Worried dull orange ache." The reminder is a word or simple phrase you'll repeat with each point to help you focus.

The irony of EFT is that often it's so effective we forget where we started. The best way to track your progress is by using what's called the SUDS (Subjective Units of Distress Scale). It's particularly helpful to write down your starting number and keywords that describe your issue. If 0 was no intensity at all and 10 was the most extreme possible, how would you rate it? I tune in to the "worried dull orange ache" and give it a rating of 7. With the SUDS rated, we move to the next step.

ACKNOWLEDGE AND ACCEPT (AKA, THE SET UP STATEMENT)

The set up statement acknowledges an issue and invites acceptance. The set up has two parts. Part one states what simply is: "Even though I feel this worried, dull, orange ache in my right shoulder…" Part two offers the counterbalance: "I'm ready for this to shift."

This accomplishes three things:

1. It allows you to tune into an issue and express your truth.
2. It creates room for both negative and positive aspects, which helps to neutralize resistance.
3. It gives you an opportunity to affirm and claim how you *want* to feel.

For many new tappers, it's generally easier to define the first part than pick the second. A challenge for some folks is that the original phrase: "I deeply and completely love and accept myself" doesn't resonate. If anything, these flowery words cause more dissonance. Always use a balance statement that works for you. It's more important to use words you agree with than to force some misaligned affirmation. This is called flexing your balance statement. Ask yourself, what feels comfortable?

Here are some examples:

- I'm just acknowledging this.
- I'm open to the possibility that this can shift.
- I'm willing to love myself anyway.
- It's okay; I'm doing the best I can.
- It's safe for me to let this go.

TAP AND NOTICE

The first two parts defined the words for your reminder and set up. Now it's time to tap. With the tips of your three middle fingers, tap gently on the outer edge of the opposite hand just below the pinkie. As you tap, repeat your set up statement three times.

"Even though...(state problem), I (use any positive or neutral statement you prefer)."

Once you've completed the set up, you'll repeat the reminder as you tap through all the points. You'll find the point list in the next section.

Pay attention as you tap. Tapping is most effective when you narrow down to a specific sensation or exact detail. This is particularly crucial when dealing with a strong emotional charge. It's not necessary to go into your story. It's actually better to use a single word or phrase that sums up your issue in a neutral way. For example, I'd suggest "dull orange sensation" over "agonizing pain in my shoulder." It's wisest to tap down distress before elaborating with evocative words or unpacking more details. At the end of each round, come back to the top of your head and take a deep breath. Assess any shifts you've experienced. Re-rate the intensity on a scale of 0-10. Whenever your SUDS remains a two or higher, repeat the tapping sequence until it's down. When in doubt, repeat the same exact words, breathe and tap through the points again. Even if you don't know exactly what's going on for you or why, when you're mindful, tapping will clarify the issue.

As you tap, perhaps you'll notice details shift from the initial problem. A dull ache in your shoulder could now move to a pinching sensation in your neck. Murky orange might now be lemon yellow. This is called shifting aspects. This is when you change the words to mirror your new perceptions. However, I want to offer some clarification and caution here. It's very common for underlying issues to surface as you tap. You might start tapping on a pain in your shoulder and realize midway that you're still peeved over a conversation with your mother.

Whenever something new bubbles up, please stay with the original issue through an entire round of points. It's easy to lose track if you go off the road. You'll have a chance to incorporate new details into your next round. Adding too many issues leads to overwhelm and complicates the process. Stirring up multiple aspects just muddies the water. Stick to the basic recipe. This will allow you to track changes and thoroughly address them one step at a time.

Another frequently asked question is: "What should I say?" Whenever possible, use your own words. Tune into your mind, heart, and body. Your personal language is always the best way to access your stuff. Notice messages you're telling yourself. Notice congestion in your body. Notice thoughts and emotions that surface. Notice the sensations, colors, feelings, and images that arise. Distill your awareness down to a sentence or two for your next set-up. Choose simple reminder words and tap through your next round. Notice whatever comes up. Lather, rinse, repeat!

TAPPING POINTS

1. Side of Hand (the outside edge of your hand, below your pinkie)
2. Top of Head (the crown of your head)
3. Inner Eyebrow (just above the bridge of your nose at the edge of your eye socket)
4. Outer Eye (on your temple, just past the corner of your eye)
5. Under Eye (directly under your pupil on the ridge of your eye socket)
6. Under Nose (the philtrum, aka the groove between your nose and lip)
7. Under Lip (the space between your lower lip and chin)
8. Collarbones (the often tender spot just beneath your clavicle and above your nipples)
9. Under Arm (on the side of your upper ribs past your breast, just below your armpit)
10. Top of Head Again. Take a deep breath. Rate your intensity.

CHOOSING EXCELLENCE

Obviously, I've just shared a tip of the iceberg. You can use EFT in many different ways. There are numerous books, research studies, and articles on the subject. This chapter is meant to be a starting point. The best way to achieve excellence in your tapping is to master these basics first. Read this chapter thoroughly. Grab my illustrated resource guide over at the Wellness Universe @jennifermoore. Take your time. Get comfortable with the points. Practice tuning in to identify sensations and rating your SUDS. Breathe. Most of all, keep it simple and keep tapping.

Author of **Empathic Mastery**, Energy Healer and Master Trainer for EFT International, Jennifer Moore supports empathic, creative women. Born from a long line of world-class *Awfulizers*, Jen (as loved ones call her) spent her first thirty years struggling to control fear and psychic overwhelm. This left her exhausted, anxious, and over-medicated.

Hitting bottom, Jen sought help. With recovery, life improved. This inspired her to pursue professional skills, including a Master's degree in Psychology & Religion, Emotion Code Certification, a Shamanic Apprenticeship, and additional healing modalities. Jen brings depth and compassion to her work through a combination of finely tuned intuition, the pragmatism of a Capricorn, and a wealth of knowledge gained from more than three decades of professional experience.

Jennifer lives in coastal Maine surrounded by flowers, bees, and elderberries. She shares this paradise with her husband David, their pug Bob, a mama doe, her two fawns, a fox, and a couple of groundhogs. When she isn't writing, teaching, or working with clients, Jen loves to create customized prayer beads, play with crystals, and make flower essences.

To learn more and grab your copy of Jen's Illustrated EFT Guide, visit https://www.thewellnessuniverse.com/world-changers/jennifermoore/

CHAPTER 4

EMBRACING LIFE

STRATEGIES FOR A LIFE WELL-LIVED

by Jim Phillips, LIFE Strategist

MY STORY

It is 5:30 AM on any given day, my normal time for awakening for over 30 years. It is a time I have come to appreciate more and more as the years slowly pass. It is usually dark, quiet, very few people, if any, an occasional call of a bird or crossing of my path by a fox. It is the time I am most connected to higher guidance and receive responses to questions or solutions to the challenge of the moment.

However, it was not always this way. It began when my beloved golden retriever, Tupelo, started nudging me at this appointed hour because she wanted to go out. In hindsight, did she know something I did not? Was she aware that this was and would continue to be a sacred time for me? Since her passing, I have come to call this sacred time, "immersed in the silence of the dawn."

Most mornings, I leap out of bed between 5:00 and 5:30 AM. Okay, to be honest, I no longer leap; it is more of an unfolding that takes place as my feet search for the floor to begin the day. On this particular morning, I was consumed by how I was living my life. Things had been going fairly well; however, I felt I wasn't living up to *my idea* of what it meant to be a spiritual person.

This conflict was causing me stress. How could I write and speak on spiritual matters when I was not living up to my idea of what it meant to be spiritual? While walking, I shared my thoughts out loud to whomever or whatever was listening. As I described my feelings, I was suddenly overcome with laughter. Spirit does have a sense of humor; this was further proof of that humor.

What immediately came to my awareness was, *stop trying to be the perfect human and just be perfectly human.* My first thought was, *seriously, that's all you are going to give me?* Then it dawned on me; I am here for the experience of being human in every way imaginable. My trying to be what I believed I should be, this more spiritual person, was denying the full experience and expression of my true nature, my Divine Being, as it desired to be experienced and expressed through me and as me in my humanness.

As a result of this revelation, my work reflects this greater understanding. There is nothing we are here to do or be other than that which we are. It is the realization of who and what we are that is life's purpose.

THE DANCE

Sunlight filters through gently swaying branches keeping time to the rhythm of a gentle breeze. Music is faintly heard as two ethereal figures move towards one another as if floating on air. Playing out in slow motion, the anticipation of the embrace builds until it explodes in joy and laughter as the two reunite. Dancing and twirling, they are consumed by the ecstasy of the realization of one another after this prolonged separation.

Embracing life, what does this really mean? And what does it have to do with the scenario played out above? Embracing life is the willingness to receive and accept life as it unfolds, knowing that as it does, it does so for you, regardless of any appearance to the contrary. It is allowing life to be experienced in its fullness and perfection.

"Life is perfect, despite evidence to the contrary"

Resistance to life is the primary cause of stress and suffering in our lives. It is the denial of all life has to offer. It is self-denial, the suppression of that which desires to experience and express through us and as us. It is the effort exerted to be other than who and what we truly are. Resistance to life hinders the realization of our truth, and therefore, the living in full expression of that truth.

Life is limitless in what it offers as our experience. It is always unfolding in our favor. Life is an equal opportunity experience, and as such, denies nothing to anyone. We are all given what is required to fulfill life's purpose. However, we all too often try to create and live life as we think or believe it should be, instead of embracing it as it is in its perfection.

> *"Life is everything we want, everything we don't want,*
> *and yet everything we need."*

Have you considered the effort put toward living up to expectations of who or what you should be placed upon you by yourself and others? Doesn't it stand to reason life would be simpler to just be who you are? Of course, this begs the question, "Who are you?" The truth is, you cannot be other than that which you are, no matter how hard you try or how much you deny this simple truth.

Notice I did not say life would be *easier* by embracing life and the truth of who we are, just *simpler.* Life will always present what is required to fulfill life's purpose, including that which we label "challenging." Life's purpose is the realization of the truth. We get to that realization through the beliefs we hold, our choices, actions we take, and experiences resulting from those actions.

Our resistance to life often flows from our overall perspective on life. Albert Einstein famously stated, "The most important decision we make is whether we believe we live in a friendly universe or a hostile universe." How the question is answered determines in large part how life unfolds.

In an interesting and unconscious way, an agreement is entered into of how life should unfold. We then proceed to attract, gather, and call to our self, evidence that supports that to which we have agreed. It is a form of confirmation bias that is insidious in nature. It is the tendency to favor information that confirms existing beliefs or hypotheses, whether or not true.

The question is now, *"How do I move from resistance to allowance?" What is the key to being released from this self-imposed prison?"* Before delving into specific strategies, I find it useful to set a realistic expectation of how life will unfold. Too often, people think if they follow certain strategies or live a certain way, life will somehow become easier and present fewer challenges, and when it does not, they feel they have failed.

The truth is, life will present exactly what we require to fulfill life's purpose, even experiences we call challenging. Once we accept this truth, a challenging opportunity is seen for what it is, something intended for our benefit, not as a cause of suffering or to hold us back.

> *"Life always presents what is required to bring about what is needed for the fulfillment of life's purpose."*

Life does not present challenges for the experience of the challenge. It presents them for the joyful experience of rising above them. When we recognize and accept this, we are more willing to embrace life for everything it presents, regardless of the outward appearance of what is presented.

THE ROLE OF FEAR IN EMBRACING LIFE

Many aspects of fear prevent us from fully embracing life. There are two most prevalent—first, fear of the truth of what we might discover about our Self. As we realize our Self as a limitless Divine Being, we fear how truly powerful we are and the responsibilities inherent in that realization. Every excuse we held as to why we cannot be or do something becomes invalid.

Secondarily is the fear of losing our self, our relationships, and life as we know it. There is the belief that if we fully embrace life all hell will break loose. In truth, this is the point. The hell we experience in life is the hell we so dearly cling to.

What I know to be true is that nothing is lost that is required for the full experience and expression of our truth. Yes, some people will no longer be a part of our everyday life; however, that does not mean we will be alone. We may no longer have experiences to which we have become accustomed. However, we will have experiences we never thought possible. We may no longer do what we have previously done; however, we will see opportunity to which we were previously blind. We will gain freedom from the fear of uncertainty as we step into the realm of possibility.

THE TOOL

STRATEGIES FOR A LIFE WELL-LIVED

1. **Understand your current reality.** This is the starting point for change. Do not concern yourself with your circumstances; concern your Self with your potential. You can look back on what you believe created the circumstances, or you can accept that regardless of what took place, this is where you are. You can be grateful for all you have, or you can lament what you believe you need but do not have.

Once we accept our current reality for what it is, we can ask some simple questions that allow us to move on. However, the key is to be brutally honest with ourselves. *What can I do? What am I willing to do, to bring about the experiences I desire?* Current reality is what *is* in the present moment, not what will be forever.

The power inherent in each moment is the power to choose how life unfolds from that moment forward.

2. **Be open and receptive to all life has to offer.** A simple strategy, yet one that can be difficult to implement—being open and receptive means releasing anything and everything that prevents the living in full expression of our truth and allowing in all that does. Life is our benefactor; let it be just that.

Releasing includes limiting thoughts, beliefs, and ideas of what life should be and how it should unfold. Limiting thoughts and beliefs of who we are, what we are deserving of, and what is possible. Life does not discriminate. It is an equal opportunity experience that provides everything required for each incarnated Soul to realize the truth of who and what it is.

*"Open your Self to receive all life is presenting
and be given all life has to offer."*

Admittedly, sometimes what shows up is uncomfortable or takes on the appearance of hardship. And yet, once we have moved beyond the experience, we realize how meaningful it was. Not that we would want the experience again, but we gained the inherent benefit. Life favors us. It does nothing to us; it does everything for us.

Life is what life is and will always be. Let go of opinions and expectations of others, especially those that deny you the fullness of life and the full expression and experience of who you are. Opinions are nothing more than a reflection of the beliefs, fears, and prejudices of the people that hold them. Detach from anything that denies you the full experience and expression of your true Self.

3. **Identify your life perspective.** Is it hostile or friendly, are you a victim or beneficiary? The way you view life is how you respond to life. How you respond to life determines how you experience life. Your experience of life reflects who you believe your Self to be. Life responds to whatever you put into the world as an expression of who you believe yourself to be. Life is compelled to do this; therefore, it can be no other way.

If you believe yourself to be a victim, life will provide every opportunity required to fulfill that perspective. If you believe yourself to be a beneficiary of life, all the goodness of life you require to fulfill that perspective is provided.

4. **Be responsible for your inspirations.** Inspirations are nudges from the Soul of what it desires to experience and express. They are one of the more powerful methods through which we realize who we are and what we are here to create and experience. Being responsible to our inspirations is to honor them, giving the attention and intention required for them to be fully realized.

When we deny our inspirations, we deny that which desires to experience and express through us and as us the opportunity to do so. Denying our inspirations is one of our greatest resistances to life, and therefore, a primary cause of suffering and stress.

5. **Unabashedly be you without fear of judgment or reprisal.** Allow that which you are to experience and express through you and as you. What is it that desires to be expressed?

> *"I Am who I Am,*
> *Always have been and will be.*
> *Who I Am is who I Am*
> *And will not change.*
> *It is who I believe my Self to be*
> *that changes to reflect who I AM,*
> *So I Am who I Am"*

6. **Give in to life.** This does not mean surrender and give up. Giving in to life is to allow, to accept, to invite, to embrace all life presents. It is making oneself available to life in all of life's expressions.

The Sufi poet and mystic Rumi said, *"What you seek, seeks you."* In essence, by embracing life, life embraces you. When chased, it is elusive; when given into, it flows to and through you.

7. **Be vulnerable.** Vulnerability is not weakness; it is extreme courage and strength. To be vulnerable is to allow oneself to be exposed in their "nakedness," in and as their truth. In vulnerability, we are defenseless. Not in the sense we are subject to being attacked and harmed, but in the sense that our defenses are dropped, thus revealing our true Self. It is through vulnerability we are more open and receptive.

8. **Be as a child.** Be curious, playful, joyful, and in awe of life in all its expressions. Shed the misconceptions of life that have been gathered through the years. Return to the innocence and truth that was known and experienced when younger. As Bob Seger once sang, *"I wish I didn't know now what I didn't know then."* (Against the Wind)

9. **Live with joyous expectation** that everything you require to realize your truth and fulfill life's purpose is provided. Trust in your Self, trust in life. Release the expectation of what you believe life should be to allow what is.

10. **Give yourself permission.** The only thing between you and the life experiences you desire is you. Give yourself permission to receive and benefit from all life has to offer. Receiving all life has to offer does not diminish what is available to all others. Life is infinite in its ability to provide all required for each Soul to gain what is intended during this lifetime. As you give yourself permission, you simultaneously give others permission.

11. **See beyond what lies before you.** The initial response to this might be to look ahead, forecast, or imagine. However, what is meant is to look at what is being perceived with different eyes. View life through the lens of clear-sightedness not blinded by the lens of fear-sightedness.

12. **Be present in each unfolding moment.** This is where truth lives. It is the only time anything can be done about anything. Realize the power and potential in each moment. Believe that what you desire to create and experience is possible. The power in each moment lies in your ability to choose. Choose wisely.

"Life is the autobiography we write as we live it.
Be careful you are not so attached to what has been written
that you are not present to what you are writing."

WHERE THIS ALL STARTED

With eyes closed, allow the scene at the beginning of this writing to unfold. The figure on the left, your Divine Self. The figure on the right, your Human self. Watch as they move through the experiences of life that were required for this union to take place. Watch as they come together in recognition of one another. Experience the joy and ecstasy of this Divine union as your Divine Self enfolds your human self with unconditional love.

Embracing life fully, irrespective of how it unfolds, is what brings about this Divine union. It is this Divine union that culminates in the realization of the truth of who we are. Living in and from this truth provides the inner peace and calm that allows us to move through and beyond any experience that would cause our stress and suffering.

"You are that which you seek."

Jim Phillips is a LIFE Strategist, author, and speaker. For over 30 years he has inspired others to higher levels of achievement and understanding through strategy sessions, coaching, and writing. One of Jim's gifts is his ability to help others understand and apply spiritual concepts to their personal life resulting in a greater understanding and experience of who they truly are. His work has been featured on CBS, NBC, ABC, FOX, and hundreds of nationally-syndicated television, newspaper, and magazine outlets.

Jim has written two books, *The Key to LIFE; living in full expression,* published by Sacred Stories Publishing, and a self-published book, *From Inspiration to Intention.*

Jim is a featured expert in the transformational movie, "Becoming the Keys," that also stars such notables as don Miguel Ruiz (Four Agreements), Dr. Joe Vitale (The Secret), and Dannion Brinkley (Saved by the Light).

At age thirteen, Jim had a profound experience that confirmed he had a very specific message to share about our connection to the Divine and our Divinity. This message was to be shared when the time was right; that time is now.

Jim resides in Brambleton, VA, where he continues writing, coaching, and speaking.

https://www.thewellnessuniverse.com/world-changers/jimphillips/

CHAPTER 5

NARCISSISTS, GASLIGHTERS, TOXIC RELATIONSHIPS, OH MY!

IDENTITY, MANTRA, AND JOURNALING FOR EMPOWERMENT IN TOXIC RELATIONSHIPS

by Laura Ellick, Ph.D.

MY STORY

Being in a relationship with this man is a lot like trying to escape quicksand: the more you try to fight it, the more it envelops you until you eventually give up and let it drown you. This thought repeated in my head as I left my house to go to work. However, I wasn't quite sure how I would be able to focus on my work; my head was spinning, and I felt the familiar feelings of anger, frustration, hurt, and confusion. Oh my God, the confusion! It was difficult for me to understand how I, a psychologist for many years, could not hold a conversation or have a "discussion" with my partner without coming out of it feeling crazy, agitated, and with the idea that something wasn't "right." All I knew was that I saw a woman who was bone tired, sad, and completely lost when I looked in the mirror every day. The woman who was once an adventurer and filled with optimism and energy was a shell just going through the motions and trying to survive day by day. I had long ago stopped dreaming because I no longer had thoughts or feelings that belonged to me. I was repeatedly told that I was "an angry, angry woman" who was not appreciative of all that my husband gave me, that I was constantly attacking him and rejecting him. At the same time, everybody else loved him, respected him, and believed that I should be grateful to be married to such an amazing guy!

Gaslighting is a specific form of manipulation used by narcissists to get control over their partner. The term comes from a 1938 play in which the main character tries to convince his wife that she is insane to get access to her money. One of his strategies is to lower or raise the gaslights in their house and then feign ignorance when his wife questions anything different about the lighting. This, along with other "tricks," convinces the wife that she is going crazy. In other words, the goal is to cause the victim to doubt her own reality enough so that the gaslighter has total control over her. Of course, in the movie, she gets the last laugh, but I won't ruin it for you.

In reality, narcissistic individuals feel very much out of control, exhibit a lack of empathy, have trouble with being vulnerable in relationships, and need to be admired and told that they are "perfect." Narcissists will go to extremes to uphold their fragile sense of self. While narcissistic and gaslighting relationships occur between parents and children, bosses and employees, and friends and coworkers, it is particularly difficult when romantic partners are involved. "Home" is supposed to be a safe place and a haven from the outside world, but often winds up being a place of confusion, drama, and manipulation. Unfortunately, one member of the partnership (usually the female half of the pair in a heterosexual relationship) lives an incredibly stressful existence, stripped of individuality, and convinced that there is something wrong with her. A narcissist will think nothing of throwing his partner under the bus to make him look better to the outside world. Image is everything, and the narcissist needs to present a "good guy" facade to friends, neighbors, and colleagues. A narcissist will go to extremes to help out an acquaintance while leaving those closest to himself to fend for themselves. Cultivating this image of the "guy who can do no wrong" is cunning: Nobody will ever believe it if his partner says something negative about him, because he is so "great" and she is so lucky to have him.

After 15 years with my partner, I was incapable of making any decisions around him because everything I said was countered and questioned to fit his world view. At the beginning of our relationship, he would ask for my opinion on paint color or re-modeling options for our home, but would then convince me that I was wrong and that his ideas were better. A typical strategy would be to say, "But don't you think it would look better if…" or "Really?! We should…" Finally, I got to the point where I gave up expressing my view and even said to him, "Why do you even ask for my opinion since you will do what you want anyway?" After several years more of this steamrolling on every topic you can think of (dinner choices, child-raising strategies, my career, etc.), I would start to cry if I was asked my opinion about something because I had no ideas of my own. I dreaded having to discuss a couple issue with my spouse because I knew it would be a good 30 minutes or more of chipping away at my viewpoint until we came to *his* conclusion. Every conversation led to anxiety, a pit in my stomach, and a headache. The stress was affecting me on every level, physically, emotionally, and spiritually.

I knew that to get healthy enough to make a clear-headed decision about my marriage, I was going to have to develop a tool (or two) in my back pocket to pull out immediately when I was dealing with him. I needed to manage the stress of this relationship in the moment so that I wouldn't get derailed during conversations with my partner. My goal at that time was not to challenge his view or convince him that I was right; I was simply looking for a way to manage the stress of these conversations so that I could continue with my day without being significantly affected. In addition, I knew I needed to heal from the trauma to get "me" back.

The fact that I am a psychologist means that I can find really cool gadgets, books, and toys in places that other people don't have access to because of the nature of my job. However, the most valuable tool for stress relief that I use was something that I stumbled upon at the Holocaust Museum in NYC about ten years ago. I was attracted to a colorful magnetic board because of the giant magnet at the top: "What do you stand for?" When I first saw it, I couldn't remember what I stood for; heck, I couldn't even figure out what I wanted for dinner. Below the giant magnet were about 35 smaller magnets with core values and traits on them, such as "Justice," "Courage," and "Integrity." At some point in the long-ago past, I knew that I had been a creative thinker. When I started reading all of the traits listed on the board, I had some foggy memories of dreams and qualities I was proud of in the past. I bought the board and ran with it. I had figured out what I needed to clear my head, function better, and manage the stress.

My goal is to share what I developed so that others in similar relationships can manage their stress too! There is a small amount of background prep, but once that is done, you can use this tool at any time, even during those interactions with the narcissist/gaslighter that leave your head spinning.

THE TOOL

1. First off, make sure you have a journal on hand that speaks to you. This is super important because you are beginning the process of finding yourself, rediscovering your interests, and remembering who you are. Give yourself the gift of time and allow yourself the experience of sorting through a selection of books and journals to see which one fits you. After you have found an appropriate journal, you can pick words from the following list (or Google "empowering words") and create a sheet that can be cut and pasted into your journal, so it looks something like this:

Kindness	Love	Empowered
Creativity	Humor	Sensitivity
Loyalty	Wise	Intuitive
Thoughtful	Grounded	Smart
Leader	Outgoing	Motivated
Optimistic	Positive	Dynamic
Responsible	Driven	Direct
Authentic	Brave	Caring

2. Feel free to use this list (or create your own) to create a mission statement or statement of identity. This statement is going to be your guiding mantra but may change as you change and evolve. For example, a mission statement might be, "I am a smart, creative, and positive woman who is sensitive and loving. This is who I am." Whenever you journal, write this statement at the top of the page as a reminder of who you are and what you stand for. Repeat this statement to yourself multiple times a day and practice feeling into what each quality represents for you. Knowing this identity statement is the key to managing the immediate stress and anxiety of being in the vortex of confusion and manipulation with the narcissist in your life.

Whenever you begin to speak with your narcissist and he causes you to question your reality: *Am I really selfish? Did I truly forget to mention to him that it was his turn to pick up the kids?* Take a breath, and repeat your mission statement to yourself. Doing so will immediately ground you and remind you of who you are and how you present in the world, in spite of what your gaslighter is telling you.

Next, go to your journal and circle (or write) the words that describe you and are relevant to this particular conversation. In this situation, I would circle "Responsible," and "Caring," and write in "Giving." The goal is to prevent you from taking the bait and getting overwhelmed by the anxiety and stress of dealing with the narcissist's manipulation and inability to take responsibility for his actions.

Once you start using this tool, you will find that your ability to manage anxiety during conversations with the gaslighter in your life will become much better. As with any strategy, using it consistently is key. Take time while you are driving in the car to think about your identity mantra, to repeat it, and to evaluate it. Do this frequently to see if it still fits you as you continue to grow. Over time, you will become more confident in yourself and in your ability to stay grounded during conversations with toxic individuals.

Laura Ellick, Ph.D., is a New York and Florida licensed psychologist and the owner of Dr. Laura Ellick, Psychology & Wellness Services, P.C. She has over 20 years of experience working with child, adolescent, and adult patients with diverse needs, such as eating disorders, medical illnesses, depression/anxiety, and trauma. She is the author of *Total Wellness for Mommies* and the just-released *Wisdom from the Universe*. She is also a coach and speaker and runs online and in-person workshops and courses to empower women to lead their best lives. Dr. Laura is certified in Reiki and Zumba and strongly believes in the mind-body link and its impact on health and wellness. She has a passion for foreign languages and travel and has lived with families in both Mexico and Ecuador to study and volunteer. She is also the mom of three amazing kids and aspires to teach them all to be leaders and not followers.

For more information, you can find Dr. Laura at The Wellness Universe website at: https://www.thewellnessuniverse.com/world-changers/drlauraellick/

CHAPTER 6

MINDFUL NUTRITION FOR MENTAL WELLBEING

CHOOSING FOODS
TO HELP LIFT YOUR MOOD

by Linda Gillan

MY STORY

In 1993, I experienced a sudden episode of mental illness, resulting in traumatic admission to a hospital psychiatric ward, with a diagnosis of *'Brief Reactive Psychosis.'* This was the first of three such episodes, triggered on each occasion by long term, unresolved, emotional stress. During this first incident, as I lay in the hospital emergency room, I was a witness from the inside looking out, as my world fell into deeper disorder around me. I felt frightened, disorientated, and exhausted. Once in the ward, all I know is, for several days, I slept a lot. Then I woke up one day and remember thinking, *I'm back*. My head nurse was amazing, she gave me a cassette player and a music tape, Tony O'Connor—Mariner. A few days later, she gave me a book and said, *"You might like to read this."* Scott Peck—The Road Less Travelled. As the days passed, I gradually began to feel stronger, venturing out for short walks and meditating every day. I also enjoyed eating again.

This was a time of big changes and readjustment in my life, and several weeks later, I was discharged from the hospital with prescribed medication for anxiety and depression. In recovery, I noticed certain foods I ate seemed to affect my mood positively.

Over the next few months, I had strong food cravings and found that eating these foods made a big difference to how I felt, some making me feel significantly brighter, with more clarity and focus. I followed the urges for these cravings and began to see distinct patterns in reactions to my mental state.

I kept a daily journal for two years and researched the foods that I felt were creating a positive change in my mood, noting specifically what I was eating throughout the day and how I felt afterward. I spent hours plowing through library books (in the days before Google was king), and my main mode of research was trial and error, with some good experiences and some not so great. I cut out alcohol and caffeine drinks, substituting with herbal teas.

It was a hot Australian summer, and I discovered the importance of keeping hydrated. I had frequently overlooked drinking enough water and found that being even slightly dehydrated made my mental and physical energy levels drop, and my mood slump. After having a drink, the turn-around was remarkably quick in making me feel less lethargic, brighter, and more alert. I learned that it is important to drink plenty of water or keep hydrated with unsweetened beverages, whatever the climate. Other fluids came from eating fresh fruit and vegetables and re-hydrating foods that absorb their cooking water: pasta, porridge, rice, and soups.

Under medical supervision, I gradually lowered my medication levels. I explored natural therapies and energy medicine, finding great benefit in Kinesiology, Re-iki, and Flower Essences. All the while continuing to monitor my diet and mental wellbeing.

I continued to record my trials and tribulations, and distinct patterns showed up in gauging how specific foods made me feel, some relieving mental fatigue and others lifting my mood and easing anxiety. On the other foot, some foods made me feel heavy and lethargic, and I quickly learned to avoid processed foods and sugar. High on the list of positive results were foods rich in B-vitamins, magnesium, antioxidants, and Omega-3, plus foods providing good sources of the amino acid Tryptophan, which produces serotonin, the 'feel-good' brain chemical.

Often, I would devour a big bowl of porridge, or eggs cooked in any fashion for breakfast. I found myself reaching for bananas, tinned salmon, spinach, blueberries, honey, plain yogurt, and dark chocolate throughout the day. I later learned that these all had many benefits to lift the mood and increase mental function. I munched away on fruit and nuts at any time of day or night, and Popeye would have been proud of my insatiable appetite for spinach! I drank green tea or chamomile and ate sensible sized portions of meals, making sure to balance all food types. I figured, if my body was madly craving a particular food, there was most likely something in it that I needed.

THE TOOL

This is a list of some of the foods I found beneficial. Emerging research in neuroscience is showing a distinct link to the gut-brain connection and mental health.

- NATURAL YOGHURT contains healthy bacteria. Yogurt and other fermented foods can benefit the natural gut bacteria and positively affect brain health.

- BEE HONEY contains strong antioxidant properties and a wide range of compounds that counteract oxidative stress and help shift an anxious or low mood.

- FATTY FISH, such as salmon, tuna, herring, trout, sardines, and mackerel, provide oxygen to the brain and help neurons move easily throughout the brain. Fatty fish are high in Omega-3's and help balance the mood. Salmon and sardines are sources of vitamin D, which regulate the immune system and support brain function.

- NUTS and SEEDS are high in Tryptophan, vitamins, and antioxidants. They are excellent brain food to help calm the mind and elevate mood. Nuts, especially almonds, are an excellent source of vitamin E. Brazil nuts contain selenium, reducing inflammation and can help ease anxiety. One or two brazil nuts a day helps keep a low mood at bay.

- DARK BERRIES – blueberries, cranberries, mulberries, and blackberries are a fantastic source of antioxidants and polyphenols, a great boost for digestion and improve brain health.

- ASPARAGUS, aka 'the happy plant,' is high in folate and a great source of Tryptophan for serotonin, helping lift the mood.

- BANANAS are a conveniently packaged food with vitamin B6, folic acid, and essential minerals such as Calcium, Phosphorus, Potassium, and Magnesium, providing a burst of energy and calming the mind.

- AVOCADOS are a 'fatty fruit' containing monounsaturated fat. They produce healthy blood flow and brain health. They are a high source of B vitamins: good stress relief and energy boosters.

- DARK CHOCOLATE (min 70% cacao). YES! Good news, not only does it taste good, one of the benefits of dark chocolate is it contains Tryptophan for producing serotonin. Eating a few pieces can help lift the mood.

- LEAFY GREEN VEGETABLES are packed with micronutrients, fiber, and vitamin C. Spinach contains Tyrosine, Tryptophan, vitamins, minerals, and magnesium. Greens help with brain health and mental alertness.

- PUMPKIN SEEDS contain manganese, magnesium, phosphorus, and zinc, all of which help elevate mood and energy levels.

- LEAN MEATS For the meat-eaters: Turkey, pork, lean beef, and chicken are good sources of protein and vitamin B-12. These meats provide Tyrosine, an amino acid that promotes mental clarity and alertness.

- QUINOA is rich in amino acids, is packed with protein, and provides folate, magnesium, phosphorous, and manganese for brain function and a boost of stamina.

- BEANS are a complex carbohydrate, providing protein and energy for the body and brain, resulting in improved mental focus and energy.

- BROWN RICE is a powerful antioxidant and may help balance the mood and maintain healthy brain function.

- APPLES are great for body and mind. They are high in antioxidants and contain Quercetin (most of which is found in the skin). Quercetin is believed to protect the brain cells from oxidative stress and improve brain health.

- OATS are a slow-release, highly nutritious food, containing B-vitamins for a healthy mind and body.

- EGGS are a great source of protein and Omega-3 for brain health and mood lift. They are rich in vitamins and minerals and contain the amino acid Tryptophan which produces serotonin. The yolks provide vitamin D, supporting brain function.

- HERBAL TEAS are high in antioxidants and many other health benefits. Some teas have anxiety relief properties. Two of my favourites are green tea and chamomile.

- GREEN TEA contains L-Theanine, which produces Serotonin and Dopamine, which in turn, send messages between nerve cells in the brain, which can help lift the mood and increase cognitive function.

- CHAMOMILE is an antioxidant and anti-inflammatory, containing flavonoids which can help to calm and relax the mind and body

On the topic of tea. When I felt very anxious, I found the simple act of making a cup of tea helped me settle. It gave me something to focus on, and holding the warm cup was very soothing. A hot drink often helped settle my jittery stomach. I later connected the tea-making process to a popular grounding technique, which brings awareness to the five senses; sight, sound, smell, touch, taste. It also possibly rekindled a part of my British heritage, where a cup of tea is the answer to everything. "I'll put the kettle on."

Recent research in neuroscience and mental health has highlighted the gut-brain connection. The bacteria in the gut are known as micro-biome and affect brain health by sending messages through nerves to neurotransmitters in the brain. Serotonin is an antidepressant neurotransmitter, mostly produced in the gut.

Some foods contain *Probiotics*, which are live, beneficial bacteria, naturally created by the process of fermentation. Other foods stimulate the growth of *Prebiotics* a non-digestible part of foods that encourages healthy bacteria. Eating foods with probiotic or prebiotic ingredients may help restore balance in the gut and improve brain health. Probiotic-rich foods include - plain yogurt, cottage cheese, fresh sauerkraut, kombucha, apple cider vinegar, and miso. Prebiotic-rich foods include artichokes, bananas, asparagus, oats, and apples.

WELLNESS is not necessarily the lack of dis-ease or illness; rather, it is how we manage life's challenges in an holistic way and function in our lives in true alignment of heart, mind, body, and spirit.

Along with maintaining a healthy and balanced diet, I encourage nurturing a positive mindset and making time for quiet contemplation for self-care. Meditation and time in nature are important aspects of my mental wellbeing, and I find exercise energizing and mood changing. It's amazing the difference even a short walk can make. I take along my drink bottle and a few nuts or a banana to nibble along the way. This takes me back to my younger years, walking and dreaming on the banks of the River Thames in Oxford, where I'm sure I once caught a glimpse of the white rabbit hopping by.

My mental illness episodes were a significant catalyst for personal transformation and spiritual awakening, resulting in massive changes in myself and my life. I have never looked back and continue to grow. Having felt great benefit from energy medicine, I later studied Usui Re-iki and Australian Bush Flower Essences to help others. My personal development resources and services are built on practical insights and strategies gained from my experiences. Many of the coping skills, tools, and strategies I used in recovery, still serve me well today, particularly in times of uncertainty and change.

I regard wellness of our entire being as a complete package, with mental, physical, emotional, and spiritual wellness deserving equal respect, understanding, and support. True wellness lies in being mindful of the quality of food we eat and maintaining a mental diet of a positive mindset and being fully aligned in our thoughts, words, and actions every day. Ultimately, we are each accountable only to ourselves for our self-care and wellbeing. Choose wisely.

Some choices and decisions

Are just too hard to make

But YOU will make the right ones

For your very own heart's sake.

There's a little voice inside you

Just like a wise old owl and

He / She will know just what to do

When things are looking foul.

There is no right or wrong way

Just the path you choose to take

No-one to condemn you

For the choices that you make.

So, when you feel you've faltered

Or got stuck along the way

Go back and ask your wise old friend

To guide you come what may.

-Linda Gillan (2001)

Linda Gillan is an international mental health advocate, mentor, and author, speaking from lived experience to bring better understanding to families, friends, and the wider community, to help make a dent in STIGMA of mental illness. Linda was born in the UK and lives in her adopted home of Western Australia. She is no stranger to change, having navigated huge personal shifts on many levels and big geographical adjustments over the years. She respects the importance of self-care and continues to use tools and strategies that were a big part of her recovery in maintaining ongoing mental health and wellbeing. Linda is the owner of HEART of LINDA | MUD to STARS project for mental health. She is the author of *'Breaking Free – Believe In Yourself As Much As I Believe In You'* and *'Inside Looking Out– mental health, spirituality and everything in between'* (upcoming memoir). Her greatest joy is seeing people of all ages and backgrounds claim their authenticity and shine their true light.

Linda Gillan, Mental Health Advocate. Dip. Mental Health.

https://www.thewellnessuniverse.com/world-changers/lindagillan/

Disclaimer: The information in this chapter is based on Linda's personal experience. Please do not stop taking prescribed medication or alter a specific diet plan recommended by your doctor or wellness professional.

CHAPTER 7

EFFECTIVE DECISION MAKING

ELIMINATING CONFLICT AND CONFUSION

by Melissa Jirovec, Mindset Strategist

MY STORY

I'm not good enough. That thought bounced around in my mind nonstop, from my early teens until I was 23 years old. I had absolutely no clue who I was, what I wanted, or where I wanted to go, but what I did know was that my grades were never great, no matter how hard I worked. My body was never right. My friendships were superficial, and I craved connection. I wasn't a good-enough figure skater to be an athlete, and that had been my dream. I doubted my every move and struggled to make decisions for fear of making mistakes and being criticized.

Then the universe stepped in with a sudden, major course correction.

In June of 2014, I was about a year into my career as a Registered Nurse, a job I was quickly learning I didn't have the nerves for. Just as I was finishing up a nightshift in the small-town hospital I worked in, we got a call that two victims of a collision were coming in, and one was in critical condition. I quickly headed over to assist in the ER for the first time, and I was so nervous that all I could think on the way there was: *Please don't let me screw this up.*

When I got there, I joined the other nurse in the unit, and we started to take a look at the critical patient. As I learned in school, I started at the head and immediately noticed that his head was so swollen, he must have a head injury. As I made my way down, I noticed an injury to the right hand and wrist, lots of torn clothing and scrapes, a broken femur, and *wait a second...*

I know those feet. It was an odd thought, but something was familiar to me. And when I looked again, I realized I knew those clothes too. My gaze slowly went back up to the patient's head, and the whole world stopped at that moment. I couldn't hear, I couldn't smell, I couldn't breathe, I couldn't feel anything. It was my fiancé.

In the span of just a few seconds, my entire life was changed.

My fiancé suffered a traumatic brain injury, amongst many other injuries. As his common-law partner, I had to make many serious decisions for him. I got a lot of love and support, but I was also pressured and flooded with negativity from people trying to be 'realistic.' Eventually, I was on my own as we moved from hospital to hospital for his care.

Do you know what I learned? How to trust me. I got a giant crash course on it. I also learned how to stand up for myself and how to truly be an advocate for someone else. I discovered my strengths, my resiliency, and the fact that I am actually not only adequate but quite capable.

It was a revelation.

When my fiancé-turned-husband was finally discharged from the hospital five months after his accident, I began a self-discovery journey while I cared for him at home. I gradually identified the things that I wanted and the things that I wanted to do. And do you know what I discovered?

Making decisions is EASY when you know who you authentically want to be, what you want, and where you're going.

So I made a committed decision.

I decided I would continuously set a big goal for myself and work towards it until I made it. I started with a vow-renewal ceremony (my husband and I were married in the hospital) and then the honeymoon of our dreams in Australia (we'd both always wanted to go). What followed was a half-marathon, self-publishing my first book, self-publishing my second book, numerous speaking engagements, and trips to Nevada, New York, Arizona, and California. Then we realized our dream of having a family, bringing two little babes into the world 20 months apart. I then competed in two bikini bodybuilding competitions, found and bought our dream home, and now I'm training for a half Ironman Triathlon while building a business I'm passionate about and contributing to this incredibly powerful book.

All in six years' time.

Sometimes I wonder what that shy, fearful, stressed, self-conscious, worried, dissatisfied girl who longed for so much more but couldn't bring herself to make it happen would say, if she could see what her future held.

I wonder just how shocked she would be to know that she could comfortably speak in front of crowds. That she could raise two young children for the most part, on her own. That she could network and seek mentorship from people who make more money in a month than she ever envisioned herself making in a year, and hold her own. That she could make good friends around the world during a global pandemic.

I mean, if I could just go back and give that girl a hug! I would let her know that everything would be more than alright.

This year it became increasingly evident to me that the universe rewards action. But we can't take consistent and persistent action without first making a committed decision.

Our time, money, and energy are too valuable to waste, making moves without direction or purpose. I often think of my husband's accident as being a near-death experience by proxy for me. It was a huge slap in the face to wake the hell up. And all of a sudden, I couldn't understand why I had been living such a limited, unhappy life.

Wake up, go to work, errands, eat, TV, bed. Regularly complain that I'm tired. Say I'm going to do things that I won't do. Feel frustration and stress because deep down, I felt like *this can't be it. I know I can't have worked so hard for my university degree for this to be it, for this to be my life.* It was far from a bad life, but it was also far from the life I was secretly dreaming of.

THE TOOL

EFFECTIVE DECISION MAKING

Indecision causes a lot of stress. As a person who used to be quite indecisive, I know the suffering it can cause; the internal turmoil as you review your choices over and over. The doubt and worry that follows your every move like a shadow. The desperation as you ask everyone you know what they think you should do, directly and indirectly. The stress and heaviness you experience as you repeatedly think: *I have no idea what I should do.*

Fear of making the wrong choice.

Fear of making a mistake.

Fear of criticism.

Fear of not moving forward (while everyone else seems to be).

Many avoid decision-making at all costs. Have you ever sat in a room with a group of people, and someone asks, "Where should we go out to eat?" And in response, you hear:

"I don't know."

"I don't care."

"It's up to you."

"You decide."

"Doesn't matter to me."

"You guys pick, I'm up for anything."

And the group frustratingly does this song and dance until someone *finally* decides to make the decision. But they didn't want to. Nobody wanted to.

Did you know that the most effective people in the world make decisions quickly and stick to those decisions? They trust themselves, and they persist in the decision until the desired result materializes into physical form.

"The man of decision cannot be stopped!
The man of indecision cannot be started! Take your own choice."

-Napoleon Hill

How do you make confident, committed decisions that are always right, always beneficial, and always moving you forward?

1. Know what you truly want (eliminating confusion).

2. Know who you truly want to be (eliminating conflict).

YOUR LIFE MAP

What you'll need:

- Pen or pencil
- Paper
- Timer
- A quiet space

Sit down and roll your shoulders backward and forward a few times, then take three deep breaths. Stretch out your fingers a bit, then get ready to set a timer for ten minutes.

During these ten minutes, you will hear nothing but the pen or pencil writing on the paper and your own breath. You will see nothing but the two lists being created before you.

Now take your sheet of paper and draw a line right down the middle, from top to bottom. Once you've done that, on the left-hand side at the top, write "WANTS." On the right-hand side at the top, write, "I AM."

Here's what you're going to do.

For the first five minutes, you're going to write out everything you really want.

1. What would make your life better?

2. What do YOU really want to have?

3. What do you enjoy?

4. What would fulfill you?

5. How do you want to spend your time?

6. What do you wish you had more of?

7. What would make things easier for you?

Do not overthink this and do not think about how's, likelihoods, or any other limiting nonsense that might come up. Stay focused and just write out the ideas that come to mind. If time and money were not an issue, what would you want?

For the last five minutes, you're going to think about the person you want to be.

1. What qualities do you really want to possess?

2. How do you really want to feel?

3. If there are people you admire, what is it about them that you like?

4. What kind of person has the things you want to have?

Write these out in the present tense, i.e., I am confident, I am wealthy, I am organized, I am in control, I am at peace, etc. Once you've completed these two lists, consider them to be your life map. This is what YOU want to be, do, and have. This is where you're going. Feel free to go over these lists a few or many times, add things, edit things, make sure they are exactly what you want.

A lot of people attribute the word success to income, fame, and material items. The truth is, success means to be moving forward. Any person moving forward toward a goal is successful. If you aren't pursuing a goal, you are stuck in place. And while that may not consciously cause you stress, subconsciously, it most certainly does.

It often comes out as frustration, irritation, lack of patience, snapping at your coworkers, spouse, or the kids. It comes out as feeling burnt out, feeling stressed, feeling sad, or feeling the fear of missing out. We are goal-seeking organisms, and we thrive when we are moving towards the things that we want. We thrive when we succeed, which is when we move forward.

Take your two lists and put them somewhere where you will see them every day. Your nightstand might be a good choice. Because they are so important, feel free to put them on nice paper, frame them, make them stand out, because they are something you want to be looking at often.

Now to move forward without overwhelm, you'll want to pick one WANT and one I AM statement to start moving toward first. Maybe there are two that can be connected in some way. If you decide you want a promotion at work, and you've decided that you will be confident, well that would be a nice pairing wouldn't it?

Once you've made your choices, then comes the most important part.

Make a committed decision that you will work on acquiring these two things, starting today.

These are your goals as an individual. This is for you, for you to thrive, for you to succeed, for you to be well and fulfilled and energized with purpose.

This will also benefit the people in your life. When they see you making progress and creating positive change in your life and going after the things you want, they will be affected. They may be really happy for you, they may comment on the change in you, and they might even be inspired and want to join you!

But first, you have to commit to yourself, here and now.

When you make a committed decision, that means that you accept no results but the results you intend to get. There's no "I'll try," or "We'll see how it goes." There are no excuses or justifications. There's no procrastination, no "thinking about it," no pros or cons.

Time, money, and energy are not barriers to your wants or your growth and development. When you really want something, you make the time, you find a way to get the money, and your excitement from desire gives you the energy you need.

We all dream in secret (your wants are your dreams!). For some, their dreams are buried so deep that they start to become satisfied with the status quo. Not happy, but satisfied. Very few dream out loud, and even fewer actually make their dreams come true. The dreams get put off to some future time, under the arrogant assumption that there is ample time left, guaranteed. Or, the deepest desires are ignored, to instead be like everybody else, for fear of taking a different path. Or, perhaps the dreams are put on a shelf, never to be chased due to the faulty belief that it simply isn't possible.

Once you know what you want and who you are becoming, you know how to move forward. There's no confusion about which direction to choose. There's no inner conflict wondering what others might say or think, what could go wrong, or any of that noise. You can feel at ease, knowing that whatever comes up, you're still moving forward. And other decisions become easy to make as well! All you have to do is ask yourself:

Is this going to get me to where I'm going?

Is this going to support my goals?

Is this going to provide the self-care I need so I can be, do, and have what I want?

Is this for somebody else? If so, do I have the time, money, and/or energy to give?

Is this a priority for me and/or my family?

No? Okay, then NEXT.

Personal growth is a continuous journey; you never arrive. But one of the biggest lessons I've learned through all this is to really pay attention to my intuition and what it's telling me, rather than listening to my logical mind, which seeks to keep me in the known, comfortable territory. A few principles I live by:

- If I get an inkling to do something, I should do it, or at least look into it.
- If I truly want it, I owe it to myself to get it. That is self-love.
- If I can't believe in and trust in me, why should anybody else?
- And the big one: How can I ever expect my children to be and love their authentic selves, to seek happiness, fulfillment, success, and live life on purpose, with intention, and experience true joy, if I don't show them how?

It all starts with a committed decision.

Melissa Jirovec is a Mindset Strategist, Author, and founder of Prosperity Unleashed. She has a healthcare background, which includes several years as a Personal Support Worker and Registered Nurse, as well as certifications in Life Coaching.

Melissa has spoken to groups at the local and national level as an advocate for caregivers and individuals with an acquired brain injury. She has been a caregiver to her husband post-ABI for six years.

At present, Melissa works with individuals who have a deep desire to change themselves and their circumstances in a significant way. Her favorite areas of focus are Self-Confidence, Goal-Setting, and Persistence. She is also passionate about helping others develop healthy coping strategies that allow them to truly thrive.

Melissa doesn't just guide her clients in setting big, exciting goals and creating life-changing results, she also commits to always having a big goal in her sights and being a product of the principles she teaches. Some of these goals include diverse fitness competitions (hello half Ironman 2021!), manifesting her dream home, and authoring several books.

For more about Melissa, you can visit her Wellness Universe Profile: https://www.thewellnessuniverse.com/world-changers/melissajirovec/

CHAPTER 8

BREATHING

A 3-MINUTE PRACTICE FOR CREATING CALM IN ANY SITUATION

by Laura Sharon, MA, ACC, CDTL/CDWF

MY STORY

I couldn't breathe and pulled the car over to the side of the highway to call 9-1-1. The late afternoon rush hour had already begun, and cars whirred past. By the time the ambulance arrived, I was convinced I would die right then and there. As it turned out, a full-blown panic attack while driving (FBPAWD) landed me in the Emergency Room that day.

Stress had bitten me in the ass before on occasion, but I was always able to manage my way through it.

***

The conference room was full of colleagues and clients who were in town for a face-to-face kick-off meeting for a new project. "I need to take a break, to get out of this room," I said to myself. I looked down at the agenda only to see the formal break wasn't for another 20 minutes. My heartbeat thumped louder and louder in my ears. My palms began to sweat. *I need to leave the room NOW.* I got up and headed to the door, making sure to pull it closed behind me as quietly as I could.

About half-way down the hall to the bathroom, I realized my breath was in the tippy top part of my chest and was very shallow. I felt light-headed as I grasped the handle and pushed open the door.

The loud whoosh of the toilet flushing got my attention, and I began to think through my next move. *I have to go outside. I need to get some fresh air.*

The ride down in the elevator seemed to take forever.

By the time I crossed the lobby and exited the building, I was already calmer. I heard an inner voice gently remind me to "focus on your breath" while I deepened and slowed each inhale and exhale.

The fresh air kept the process moving, and within a few minutes, I was calm.

Doesn't everyone who juggles young kids and a career experience this?

***

Awakened by a loud gasp, which turned out to be mine, I sat bolt upright in bed. The alarm hadn't gone off. It was still dark outside. The clock read 4:45 a.m.

Am I losing my mind?

Do I have some sort of illness?

What is wrong with me?

These questions and concerns led me to get a full medical work-up.

"Your blood work and everything looks good, normal," the doctor said. "I'd like you to try a medication."

"Medication for what?" I asked.

"For anxiety," he replied.

Given I was already in therapy to heal childhood trauma and my anxiety was becoming more severe, he recommended—and I agreed to try—a selective serotonin reuptake inhibitor (SSRI).

"Don't worry; it's not addictive. It won't fix everything, but I think it will help take the edge off of the anxiety so you can function better," he counseled.

While the medication did help take the edge off my anxiety, I continued to struggle with life's day-to-day stresses and began my search for other tools to better manage life's ups and downs. That's when I learned to befriend my breath rather than try to outrun it.

I'm confident you can learn to do the same.

> *"There is one 'Super Stress Buster' that evokes the*
> *relaxation response that we widely recommend*
> *as useful for everyone, even kids.*
> *Can you guess what it is? BREATHING!*
> *That is right, simply breathing.*
> *It is free and can be practiced anywhere.*
> *The key, of course, is focused breathing."*

The American Institute of Stress

So, what is focused breathing? It is bringing attention and consciousness to your breath in such a way that you intentionally use your breath to calm your nervous system.

A simple internet search returns numerous articles on the neurophysiology and neuroscience that explains what's happening when we use focused breathing to reduce stress. The purpose of this chapter is not to recount those details, but to teach you a simple process you can begin using right now—one you can take with you wherever you go—to manage your day-to-day stresses better.

> *"Breathing well means breathing more slowly and deeply.*
> *Relax, feel your breathing, and breathe comfortably.*
> *Once aware, it naturally becomes deeper and slower."*

Ilchi Lee

THE TOOL

What you will need:

- A timer (any type will do)
- A comfy place to sit
- Just yourself

What to keep in mind: Your breath goes wherever you go. It is with you, in you, and always available to calm you during stressful situations.

GET STARTED: ROUND 1

1. Set a timer for one minute.
2. Sit comfortably. Uncross your arms, legs, ankles if possible. Put your feet flat on the floor and rest your arms in your lap.
3. With eyes open, lower your gaze, or even close them if you'd like.
4. Allow yourself to relax and settle in.
5. Press start.
6. Bring your attention to your breathing. Where do you notice your breath – at the tip of your nostrils? In your lower belly? Your chest?
7. Maintain this focus on your breath, then take one long, deep inhale and exhale through your nose. Go slowly as you breathe in and out.
8. Take another one.
9. And then one more.
10. Continue breathing like this, through the full minute, until the timer stops.

CHECK IN WITH YOURSELF

How was that? What did you notice? Were you distracted by your thoughts or mind chatter?

Mind chatter just is. When we try to calm ourselves, it's almost as if our brains want to revolt. They work against us by thinking, thinking, thinking. Know that you are not doing anything wrong. Thinking chatter is normal. It happens to everyone. When thoughts come, just name them as "thinking" and re-focus on your breath.

Let's try this again.

GET STARTED: ROUND 2

1. Set a timer for one minute.
2. Sit comfortably. Uncross your arms, legs, ankles if possible. Put your feet flat on the floor and rest your arms in your lap.
3. With eyes open, lower your gaze, or even close them if you'd like.
4. Allow yourself to relax and settle in.
5. Press start.
6. Bring your attention to your breathing. Where do you notice your breath – at the tip of your nostrils? In your lower belly? Your chest?
7. Maintain this focus on your breath, then take one long, deep inhale and exhale through your nose. Go slowly as you breathe in and out.
8. Take another one.
9. And then one more.
10. When thoughts arise, name them "thinking" and re-focus on your breath.
11. Continue breathing slowly like this until the timer stops.

CHECK IN WITH YOURSELF

Now, how was that for you? What did you notice this second time? How would you describe your level of calm at the end of this round of practice? Was the mind's chatter a little quieter? Did naming the chatter "thinking" help you to be less distracted?

Let's try this one last time.

GET STARTED: ROUND 3

Repeat steps 1-11 again, focusing solely on the quality of your breaths, both the inhale and the exhale. If needed, slow the pace of your breathing. Feel the calm spread throughout your body. Allow your breath to relax areas of tension in other parts of your body. Breathe into them.

When the timer sounds, check in with how you are feeling in your body and whether you feel less stressed.

***

Even though you've been practicing in a certain space, rest assured, this quick three-minute practice can be used anytime and anywhere. It can also be repeated as often as necessary to create more calm in any situation. When stress comes (and it will), remember to tune into your breath, and use this three-minute technique to restore calm.

"Change your breathing, change your life."

Author Unknown

Laura Sharon is the owner of Imperative Dimensions. As an executive and life coach and performance improvement consultant with over 30 years of experience, Laura uses a wholehearted approach to help clients be their best in life and work. Laura's superpower is using data combined with asking wildly open-ended questions to help people get to the heart of what matters most. She is a Certified Dare to Lead™ and Daring Way™ Facilitator (CDTL>CDWF) bringing the research of Brené Brown to life for individuals and organizations through workshops, retreats, and one-on-one coaching.

Laura's also a mom; a health educator; a lover of art, science, animals, and the beach; a blogger; and the author of *When I Lay My Hands on My Heart: Healing Through Words and Color*, a book of poetry and drawings—for therapists and other helping professionals working with trauma survivors—that chronicles how she used creativity as a tool for healing childhood trauma.

To learn more about the services Laura offers and her additional credentials, please visit https://www.thewellnessuniverse.com/world-changers/laurasharon/

CHAPTER 9

VITAL ENERGY MOVEMENT

CREATE FLOW TO BALANCE THE BODY AND CALM THE MIND

by Carole Park, Spiritual Chi Yoga Healer and Teacher

MY STORY

My first memory of yoga is my mother dragging me to yoga classes when I was 14 or 15. It was so easy for my body then as I was thin and bendy. The class participants seemed like old ladies in black leotards with a few older men. Of course, those 'old ladies' were probably the same age as I am now. It was much later when I had a successful career with a solid team of people and enviable income that I began to feel very unfulfilled and had a sense that something was missing. I felt a kind of inner emptiness that I had no idea how to fill. There had to be more to life than the stress of sales figures.

Then one Sunday, I was sitting in the bath, feeling lost and wondering where my life was going, trying to fill the gap with a bottle of wine and a magazine, when I saw an advertisement for 'tai chi for relaxation.' I swear there was a picture of an Asian lady. I decided I would give them a call. The following day I searched through the magazine, but the advertisement wasn't there. The inspiration had come from somewhere much deeper and higher. Six months later, I joined a local tai chi class, and what a culture shock! It opened me to a completely different environment. A world of floating clouds, touching water and painting rainbows.

My life transformed as I discovered more layers of energy work and layers of myself. I learned that there is far more going on than our physical body and worldly mind and that having this awareness is so important to live a healthy life. I went on to study tai chi, chi kung, yoga and meditation. I trained in counseling and as a spiritual healer. I found myself mixing with a whole new tribe of lovely, open, supportive people.

These days the pressure and expectations in life, based on personal power gain and rushing from A to B in a specific time, are things of the past. Now my lifestyle is the rich practice of these beautiful arts. The inspiration, peace, and the deep joy of sharing them is my inner fulfillment.

THE TOOL

Why are we here? How does it all work? Humans have been asking these questions ever since achieving a rational sense of 'self.' We are constantly driven to solve problems and seek answers. To understand the world and the universe, we have developed science, technology, philosophy, art, and religion. We have gazed at the forces of nature on our world and sought to control or harness them with technology, placate them with faith and ritual, and sometimes attempt to work with nature in our structured daily lives.

In response to the questions, most of the ancient faiths, including Buddhism, Hinduism, and Taoism, have discovered the universe is one inter-connected reality that we all belong to. There is no 'self' outside this universal oneness, and we cannot stand apart from it. We are all connected and linked together. Everything we see, feel, touch, and do is simply a manifestation that our consciousness has given a form to by using the energy of the universe. This vital universal energy flows through and animates all existence and is present in all of us and in all things. It is the life force that makes the sun shine, the grass grow, the wind blow, the clouds float across the sky, and the water flow around our world. It's the life force that gives us breath.

This universal life force is called prana in India, chi in China, and ki in Japan. As this vital energy flows harmoniously through the universe, it establishes equilibrium. When it flows harmoniously through us and our planet, we can also achieve a state of equilibrium.

When the balance of energy within us is disturbed, our physical, emotional, and mental health is affected just like the balance of energy in nature is upset by pollution, cutting down and clearing too many forests, diverting great rivers, over-fishing oceans, etc.

When we're feeling stressed, it's always the result of a perceived problem. Some problems are personal and seem obvious to us; for instance, we may obsess about money, sex, relationships, or a small comment someone made. Others may be the effect of a collective human problem, either small and local, or huge and global.

Some of the problems and issues that cause us to feel stress are buried deep within our subconscious mind and are much harder to connect to and deal with. We may even look fine on the surface and seem to be coping well with life, but if we look deep within, we can see that really, we are not fine at all, and this can affect us throughout all levels of our being.

In modern society, we tend to push things down or look for a quick fix, but in reality, the problems and causes of stress are still inside and eventually surface and manifest somehow. It may begin with feeling tension in our physical body: a simple headache, tiredness, joint, or stomach pain. Or it may be something far more serious.

In times of stress, the brain and physical body are affected, and our energy field is turbulent. Our energy field or chi body permeates the physical body and the emotional and mental layers. That means mental or emotional stress can gradually work its way into the physical body. This begins in our joints, and then if left unchecked works its way into our muscles, tissues, and organs and creates dis-ease. Just like water becomes stagnant if it stops flowing, our energy also stagnates if we stop moving.

We have to look beyond logic, scientific explanations, and rational intelligence and begin to retune to the universal flow that connects everything.

To eliminate stress we need to realign, move our body to release the trapped energy, and clear and transform our outer and inner energy field. Our vital energy movement helps maintain physical, emotional, and mental harmony, and this extends into everything we do.

The word yoga means to "yoke" or to bring back to wholeness. When we practice specific yoga movements, we breathe in a certain way and stretch our physical body. Similarly, we stretch and open our energy meridians and channels and hold mudras or hand gestures. This helps our chakras or energy centers to open and become clearer and stronger. We find our health greatly improved as the new, fresh prana feeds our physical body and organs. Yoga helps us release tight or blocked energy and can even be used with healing to laser target areas where we hold tension and old blockages and issues in our bodies.

The name chi kung means 'energy work' or to 'work the energy.' In chi kung, we connect with our breath and cultivate strong, pure, positive, radiant energy and harness the chi. Holding onto it, we redirect the chi and make it work for us, so we become very strong and healthy. We can direct it to specific areas of the body or organs to remove old blockages and re-energize, replacing the old energy with the new. It supports our mind, so we use it to balance our emotions and thoughts.

The name tai chi means 'grand ultimate energy.' Tai chi is more poetic and flowing. We take the chi from the chi kung practice even further and as we move, our energy field becomes even brighter and more purified. Our vibration rises, and we attract positive, pure universal energy. This naturally dissolves any negativity that we are releasing. We begin to flow with the Tao or universe and naturally harmonize with nature and the elements and our own yin and yang—feminine and masculine aspects—return to equilibrium.

We know "like attracts like." If we feel bad, it hangs around our energy field and may attract more negative energy. When we change our energy field to positive, we change our minds, and as we change our minds, our energy changes as they constantly interact.

When we have the strength, power, balance, grace, and beauty of vital energy movement, our mind cannot be negative. Rather it becomes quiet and calm so we cannot feel stressed. Stress is replaced by empowerment and a positive, uplifted, open, and creative mind. This naturally extends into our thoughts and actions then out into our life and our world. When supported by this fresh, purified chi flowing through and around all the levels of our being, it is nature's way of keeping us safe and healthy.

The uplifting vital energy work makes it much easier to engage with the loving energy of the heart. We can transcend the intellect of the mind and rely on the more devotional intelligence of our hearts. We bring a clear, happy, positive, loving intention into our daily life and all our actions.

Eventually, tai chi practitioners flow in alignment with nature and the universe. We hardly notice our body as it becomes illuminated and dances with immense brightness and joy. Our mind is open, focused, and clear and simply led by the heart. Our soul connecting with higher intelligence shines through our movement and extends from a deep center of love, light, peace, joy, and inner wisdom. It is pure meditation in motion. When we reach this harmonious flow, the concept of stress is not even a distant, fleeting memory; it's incomprehensible as we return to universal oneness.

THE TOOL

FEELING STRESSED? MOVE, AND THE STRESS NATURALLY STARTS TO DISSIPATE AND TRANSFORM!

I invite you to pause for a moment and scan through your body and watch your mind. Simply observe how you *feel*.

For the following exercises, wear loose, comfortable clothing and the first time find a quiet place to practice. A video recording of these exercises can be found through my WU profile link: https://www.thewellnessuniverse. com/world-changers/carolepark/

HEAVEN AND EARTH RAINBOW BRIDGE SEQUENCE – STRENGTHEN CLEANSE PROTECT

This is a quick energy clearing sequence. It clears your personal energy field and the space around you and lifts your mind. You can even do this sitting at your desk at work. It's very good to practice outside in nature if you have the chance. Practice as a stand-alone exercise anytime you need a boost or before you practice the accompanying sequence. It is also good to practice before and after any physical or mental exercise.

You can perform this exercise standing or seated.

Gently align your spine and connect with your breath. Make sure you are comfortable and, if necessary, slow down your breathing. Roll back your shoulders slightly to open your upper body.

Bring your hands down towards your lower abdomen or groin area, keeping your hands away from your physical body and 6 inches apart or wider. Breathe in and simply draw your hands up the front of your body, palms facing each other, as if you are drawing the essence of the earth as a pillar of light. Take them up above your head and then breathe out and slowly sweep them down around you in a wide circle to start again. As you do this, keep your shoulders and elbows relaxed and your arms slightly curved.

You create your heaven and earth rainbow bridge where you are drawing energy and power from the earth up through your chakras and energetic system, reaching into the light above and bringing it down around you. Strengthening, cleansing, and protecting yourself in beautiful, powerful circles of light and love. Do this as many times as you like. Remember, your hands are sweeping your energy field, so shouldn't touch your body.

BALANCE SEQUENCE

You can perform this sequence standing or seated.

Standing: bring your feet a little wider than hip-width and relax your knees. Pull your belly in slightly.

Extend your arms in front of you at hip level, palms facing downwards, elbows slightly bent and shoulders relaxed.

Seated: have your feet flat to the floor about hip-width apart. Sit towards the front of your chair, pull your belly in slightly and maintain a straight back as well as you can. Do your best to avoid slouching into the back of the chair or curling forwards from your shoulders. If you have a weak back you can sit further back and use the back of the chair to support you but be careful not to slouch.

Extend your arms in front of you just above your thighs, palms facing downwards, elbows slightly bent and shoulders relaxed.

Begin by observing your breath, slow it down, and have a sense of breathing in your lower body.

1. Raising the chi
   Breathe in
   Keep your arms extended and raise them to the level of your heart.

2. Grounding the chi
   Breathe out
   Push your hands back down to towards your hips and imagine you're pushing a large beach ball down into water.

3. Breathe in

   Imagine you release the ball, and it rises out of the water, pushing your hands up back to heart level.

4. Breathe out
   Push the ball back down into the water.

   Repeat at least six times. Remember to keep your elbows slightly bent and shoulders slightly relaxed.

5. Bring the fingertips of both hands to meet each other just below your navel point/belly button or sacral chakra. In chi kung, this is called Tan Tien point.

6. Breathe in

   Keep your arms slightly extended away from your body and lift your palms to your heart or heart chakra.
   Lifting earth energy to your heart. Strengthening your heart and filling it with peace, love, light, and joy. "I bring strength and peace into my heart."

7. Breathe out

From your heart, gently turn your hands and arms so your palms face out in front of you and push them forwards as far as you can, keeping your elbows slightly bent.

Extend peace, love, light, and joy out into your life and your world. "I send strength and peace to my life and my world."

8. Breathe in

Keep your hands at heart level and gently turn your hands again to face your body and slowly open your arms as though you are hugging a large beautiful tree.

Extend the peace, love, light, and joy out from your worldly self into your spiritual layers.

9. Breathe out

Palms facing downwards push your hands down and in towards your groin/base chakra area.

Pushing all this strength and healthy, positive energy down into your physical body.

Keep your palms facing downwards, move your hands outwards to your thighs but not touching them.

10. Breathe in

Raise your chi. Slowly raise your hands up to heart level, keeping them about hip-width apart.

11. Breathe out

Ground your chi. Push your hands back down to hip level.

Repeat the balance sequence as many times as you like. Aim for at least

12. Hold the sense of the earth energy rising to support and nurture you, bringing strength, balance, and calm.

Follow this with three to six of the previous Rainbow Bridge movements.

GATHERING AND STORING THE CHI

To finish, extend your arms out to the sides of your body as if you're forming a pyramid or mountain shape. Breathe in and gently raise your hands up around your body and above your head, creating a wide circle. Now breathe out, and with your palms facing downwards, push the energy down the front of your body to your sacral chakra or tan tien.

This stores the chi/prana/life force energy at your sacral chakra so you can draw on it throughout your day.

Feel free to add your own affirmations, mantras, and visualizations and play relaxing music. As you practice, your energy and mind begin to transform, and you retune to the natural rhythm of nature and the universe.

Carole Park is a dedicated lightworker. A teacher of Infinite Tai Chi, Chi Kung, Yoga, and Meditation and personally practices these arts for at least 3 hours a day. She has 20 years experience of study, teaching, and healing practice. She runs workshops and seminars, gives demonstrations and presentations as well as 1:1 sessions. Carole is a gifted channel and connects deeply with her students and clients. She will help you stand in your power, unlock your potential, and manifest your best life. Carole is qualified in Ling Chi Healing Art and developed her own Ling Chi Yoga series for bringing yoga and healing back together. She has worked extensively with the Chinese and Asian communities and helped many souls suffering from long term sickness. After an initial consultation, Carole will help design your own personalized program back to wholeness.

Carole is from and lives in the United Kingdom with her husband. You can often find her walking in the countryside surrounding Barnoldswick with her dog and creating beauty in her garden. Her favorite place in the world is Bali, where she loves the energy and feels completely at home. https://www.thewellnessuniverse.com/world-changers/carolepark/

CHAPTER 10

PEAK SPORTS PERFORMANCE MINDSET

ELIMINATE ANXIETY ON AND OFF THE FIELD

by Kim Marie Pauline, DLM, CNS, CNC, CPT, PES & CES

MY STORY

How do you leverage peak performance mindset, you ask? Well, that question took me most of my athletic career to master. You see, I was the underdog who always found a way to succeed.

From the very beginning of my existence, I suffered structural deformities due to breech birth. So here I was, a newborn baby with a metal and leather bar around and between my legs to help straighten them and my feet out. The cumbersome device kept my legs apart since they were too close together and turned in from my hips. This would help position them to grow normally.

My mother had to exercise my legs daily, but it was too painful for her, so it became my father's job. Eventually, I learned to roll myself over with the braces, stand, and walk. By the time I was five years old, I was enrolled in ballet to help correct pigeon toe, gain a turn out in my legs and feet, and have grace and balance.

I danced my way through three dance schools. Ballet, modern, jazz, tap, toe, and acrobatics consumed my time after school four nights a week. At the age of ten, the owner of the third dance company summoned my mother and me into her office and proclaimed that I would never become a prima ballerina, nor would any dance company hire me as I would stick out like a sore thumb. Mom was appalled; how dare she say that. I just said thank you for your concern; it wasn't why I am here. I do love jazz dance, though.

In that instant, I felt my heart and body sink. My CONFIDENCE was thrown off-kilter for a day or so. Then I decided to fight back. My GOALS drove my effort and will.

I developed the MOTIVATION to succeed. This was key to maintaining the love I first experienced for my sport while reaching my athletic success potential.

In junior high and beyond, I played lacrosse and soccer and ran cross country.

Beating my own personal best from day to day drove my training and built up my COMPETITIVE SPIRIT.

My love of dance never diminished. I found I was happiest on the dance floor. While at college in New York City, I continued to study modern and jazz dance.

As I got older, I found my health and weight became more and more important to my beliefs around the way I looked, felt about myself, and affected my athletic performance.

Plus, I grew up seeing my grandmother with diabetes and a leg amputation due to her inability to correct her eating habits and quit smoking. My great aunt was on dialysis in the house, another side effect of diabetes if you do not address the underlying issues causing you to disease and take medications to lower your numbers. The other side of my family suffered from heart disease and a congenital thickening of the heart wall, called Hypertrophic Cardiomyopathy, along with intestinal, colon, prostate and skin cancer.

Subconsciously, I decided a long time ago that I would not end up like most of my family regarding their health.

Comrades in the gyms I trained in kept asking me when I was going to compete in bodybuilding. I remember telling them that I couldn't compete looking like this!

I decided to hire a long-time female bodybuilding competitor to train me for my first show. We did not have the same ideals around training, as she believed that what you can't lift on your own, you can't count. I know from experience that if I'm going to hire a trainer or have a lifting partner, we are spotting each other to lift heavy enough to do forced reps and negatives to grow and push past our own personal best daily.

The first year I competed, what I was told by one of the judges at the end of the night when I asked for feedback was, "I'm not sure why you're here; either you don't have a back or don't know how to pose your back." Many people would have given up at this point, but not me. "That's bullshit," I said, **"I CAN, I WILL, I MUST."** I was able to show them how resilient I was, certain and confidant that I would overcome what I needed to.

I was bound and determined from that point on whatever I set my mind to I would frickin do.

I hired a pro bodybuilder and promoter of The Ironman Classic, in Central New York, Jeramy Freedman. I learned techniques, strategies, and routines that helped perfect my own personal best, drive training, and competition. The one thing I couldn't do was eat like him and get the same results. He competed at 307 pounds, was six feet tall, and had a 59-inch chest with 22-plus-inch arms, a giant compared to me.

I went back to college at Syracuse University, studied clinical nutrition, and then added lifestyle medicine to learn what I needed to do to get the results I was looking for to optimize my health and conditioning at the highest level.

I continued to compete, and even though I consistently made the top five lineup, I was no stranger to handling disappointments. Denise Gerard, a female pro bodybuilder and NPC judge, saw the disappointment on my face during the placing and immediately told me what I needed to focus on. She became my next mentor and contributed to my competing at the national level.

Now the pressure was on. Like a video in my mind of any contingency that might arise, I began to look at the competition and tackle any barriers or problems. You have to be careful of self-doubt because it could cause everything you've worked for to all crumble down. Insecurities may creep up on you as you question whether you're good enough and if your plans will come to fruition.

Here I was, this great achiever and still not getting things right in other areas of my life. I had to find a way to fix things. I went to therapy, and that didn't work. I found myself talking about my sad story so much that I was actually beginning to believe it even more.

I tried self-help, but that was like the blind leading the blind. Then I traveled around the world to work with the best healers, teachers, and universities to search for a solution to avoid heart disease, diabetes, dialysis, and cancers that the family endured and find out why I was sabotaging my success reach pro-athlete status. India was my first stop, and John Harricharan and Sri Vishwanath were instrumental in starting the process for me to mentally, emotionally, and physically manifest my dreams.

Sports psychology and neuro-science gave me the biggest edge when it came time for "The Underdog" to take on the best and win despite the odds.

Pre-performance routines and rituals in and out of the gym were designed to help relax, focus, and sharpen mentally, emotionally, and physically for upcoming events. When I started to implement the ones I found that worked best for me, I became a champion, and so can YOU.

I don't know if anyone has tried to keep you down or said that you couldn't do something. Or maybe you're struggling with some health problems like my family did. You may have tried self-help or therapy and thought it didn't work for you either. Through all those things I overcame and all those people who came to me to train them over my career, I've come up with a proven system.

In the short period of time we have together, I'm going to share a couple of pieces of that system with you, and later on, I'll tell you how to find out more.

THE TOOL

The WellnessBod, Body-Mind Transformation tool kit offers;

PREPARATION TECHNIQUES

- Instill mental preparation
- Teach techniques and strategies for performance
- Dealing with stress and coping with setbacks

FACTORS LINKED TO YOUR SUCCESS IN SPORTS

Motivation: Goals that define the athlete or person

- Confidence
- Performance knowledge: Total sport and "knowing the opposition."
- Routines
- Anxiety management: Getting you in the right frame of mind.
- Experience: Remind you of your experience
- Modeling: Blueprint of optimal performance
- Observation
- Imagery: Mental rehearsal
- Self-talk: Important and relevant to the event
- Feedback
- Anxiety Management: Relaxation techniques, breathing, stretching, muscles, music, meditation

If you are an athlete, you may have things you like to do ahead of your event that make you feel optimistic, confident, and energized, like a batter before they swing. This is your ritual.

If you are a businessperson making a presentation, you probably perform tasks ahead of time that contribute to your focus and organization.

If you have to make an important, difficult phone call, you should have a routine you use to keep you calm, in the proper mood and frame of mind.

Rituals are perhaps the most misunderstood and most under-used mental training tools in a performer's tool kit.

SUCCESSFUL STRATEGIES FOR DESIGNING YOUR OWN PRE-PERFORMANCE RITUALS

1. Imagery: Watch your best performances and visualize your success at the event

2. Read your mental training journal for evidence of past successes

3. Use positive self-talk

4. Relaxation right before your event (meditation, or music)

5. Make an overall game plan

6. Seek support staff to reduce pressure on your self

7. Eat specific meals at specific times

8. Wear clothing that makes you feel confident

9. Check all the equipment you'll be using

10. Warm-up, stretch, and exercise everything you'll use in your performance to burn off nervous energy

11. Check out the venue where you will perform

12. Be around people who support you and make you feel confident

13. Be around people who are models of mental toughness

14. Know your opening tactics cold, so they are automatic

15. Make a back-up or emergency plan.

SHIFTING YOUR MINDSET EXERCISES—THIS IS WHERE VICTORY WILL EMERGE

Perceived stress often increases for athletes on game day because they have an audience, and they place extremely high expectations on their success.

This type of stress is often based on the way athletes interpret the situation. It is rarely the external situation that causes stress, but rather the way your self-talk describes the situation that creates feelings of stress, anxiety, and fear.

The thoughts you have about your event can be modified, adjusted, or controlled with appropriate sports psychology and mental practice. Here are a few tools that I use for myself and clients that help modify Identity, language, behavior, communication, and outcome.

Changing physiology: give yourself permission to release anxiety with your body and breath, realizing that you're always capable of growth and change.

When anxiety creeps into your day, you always have the power to step out of it. I use a progressive muscle relaxation technique that's researched-backed for lower levels of stress. It helps ground ourselves in our bodies and the world around you. When this happens, you'll find choosing what you want out of your day becomes effortless.

Mindful Breathing and movement give us the tools for our mental, physical and emotional wellbeing. They help us relieve stress, build self-awareness, and find focus.

CHANGE LIMITING BELIEFS AND NEGATIVE SELF-TALK

1. What are some of your limiting beliefs?
2. And how do they affect your life?
3. What negative consequence have you had in your life as a byproduct of your limiting belief?
4. Write ten new empowering beliefs for yourself.

Once you know what you're unconsciously saying to yourself, you can change it in a SNAP.

CHANGE YOUR LANGUAGE WITH POSITIVE AFFIRMATIONS

Write down 50 "I am" statements. Be honest with yourself, as there will be positive and not so positive.

For those not so positive, come up with empowering alternatives.

As you start your daily routine, recite your 50 I am's on a regular basis. I like to recite them naked in front of the mirror, on the stair climber, while practicing my lifting, footwork, or running.

Tolerate discomfort. You'll learn to accept feelings without being controlled by them.

Reflect on progress daily. Take time to consider what you've achieved and focus on where you are going.

MANTRAS TO THINK AND ACT PRODUCTIVELY

There are six human needs:

1. Certainty - Need for shelter, water, food, control, helplessness, always sick or playing sick to get attention.

2. Uncertainty - Variety, cooking different meals, bord in a relationship so they commit adultery.

3. Significance - Sense of being needed, important, separation, better than you, being unique.

4. Love and Connection - We will settle for connection but really want Love. Family, friends, gangs and may do things outside your beliefs to get the love and connection you need.

5. Growth - Spiritual, it's no longer about you, it's to serve others for the greater good and make a difference.

6. Contribution - Giving back or lifting others up, taking care of others

We all satisfy at least three to four of those human needs daily, on a good, bad, or indifferent level. How are you meeting your needs? Fill in the blanks to start meeting your needs in a positive, desired way.

Because I AM _____ (in the present tense state your vision of who you REALLY desire to be)

I MUST focus daily on_____ (list the primary activity – only one)

POWER POSE

How to feel and exude confidence. Posture impacts how we feel about ourselves. "High power" poses (example; Wonder Woman, Superman, tall and proud) increase confidence, while "low power" poses (example; protective, slouched, closed, and guarded) perpetuate a weak sense of self.

Try this: Before entering a social or high-pressure situation, hit a "high-power" pose for two minutes for a boost in confidence.

As a Special Bonus Offer, limited to those seriously being challenged, have tried other things that have not worked and it's time to get help. Simply fill out the form, and request a FREE Strategy Call now at https:// www.thewellnessuniverse.com/world-changers/kim-marie-pauline-ms/ activity/

CIRCLE OF EXCELLENCE EXERCISE

Visual Imagery, Preparation and Rehearsal

In this exercise, we will be anchoring a Power Move to a Peak State

You can establish an anchor quickly. Repeated motivations and conditioning reinforce an anchor.

Anchors are "set" and "fired off." The more profound the experience when the catalyst is set, the stronger the retaliatory response. Make it unique and repeat.

Examples of a Power Move

Move your body in a way that makes you feel strong and invincible. Don't be afraid to make it your own.

- It can be making a fist and shouting YES!

- Putting your hands up (with or without making noise)

- Overhead double bicep pose

CHAPTER 10 - PEAK SPORTS PERFORMANCE MINDSET | 89

- High five
- Clapping your hands rhythmically
- Pounding your chest
- Thumbs up
- Wonder Woman/Superman pose

1. ***Identify Your Desired Peak State.*** Decide upon the states or levels of excellence in your life that you desire and what state you want your resources available to you?

2. ***Who do you desire to be?*** Decide on what emotions will serve you in being that person. Decide what your reality needs to be. Decide what your identity has to be, how you need to show up, Your body, communication, direction to support your optimum self. How do you need to carry yourself, breathe, act, move? What do you say to yourself and others, how do you communicate, what tonality do you use, how do you project? What is your vocabulary? What direction are you moving toward, where are you going, where's your focus? You have the opportunity to design your optimal self.

3. **Organize a Circle of Excellence.** I want you to envision a circle of excellence right in front of you. Tell me about what it looks like to you, the colors and sounds, etc. Is there a feeling associated with it?

Elicit the desired person's attributes:

a. Global beliefs about what makes them effective

b. Key values or criteria that they use to create consistent success

c. Reference experiences that they use to make evaluations

d. Rules that they utilize

e. Evidence procedures that determine that their rules are being met

f. Strategies that they take to achieve the result (how) they take action, i.e., syntax the specific order of their strategies

g. The emotional state that they are in when taking action

4. **Access Excellence Circle.** Reflect on your life. Can you think of a specific time when you were in a completely blissful place? When you have that in your mind, close your eyes.

   a. Take a deep breath in and exhale slowly.

   b. Take another deep breath in and exhale slowly.

   c. Take one more deep breath in and exhale slowly.

   d. As it envelops you, step into that circle.

   e. Every experience or access to this tranquil spot should help you see it through your own eyes, becoming the person you desire to elicit.

   f. See what you saw, hear what you heard, and feel what you felt.

5. *Now "set" and "fire off" your Power Move*

6. *Separator State/Testing.,* Open your eyes. Come out of the circle, relax for a moment, then walk back into the circle. Anchor and discover just how completely you produce those feelings. Now, remove yourself from the circle, breathe, enjoy the moment.

7. *Desired Context.* From now on, whenever you walk back into the circle. Visualize a future situation, or set of circumstances where you want to experience or feel this exalted state.

8. *Chaining. Anchor:* I'd like you to return to the circle and recapture that exalted state. Breathe and wait a moment. Think about how precisely that old problem will be different.

Self Testing. As you leave the circle, think about where you want help. Explain the non-verbal areas.

The power is truly is in your hands. You hold the key to your success. And even where there are past concerns still plaguing you, you can control your mind and say enough is enough when it gets out of control.

Believe in yourself; *truly* believe.

Whatever you dedicate yourself to will eventually flourish and become your reality even if it doesn't look exactly like what you want.

"We are what our thoughts have made us; so, take care about what you think. Words are secondary. Thoughts live; they travel far."

– Swami Vivekananda

Kim Marie Pauline is reputed as a world-class thought leader in the health and fitness industry. As a Doctor of Lifestyle Medicine and professional athlete, she founded WellnessBod.com, cracking the code on physical and mental performance. Kim empowers achievers globally to develop and sustain the Mind, Body, and Spirit of a Champion.

Kim is renowned as a trusted fitness advisor to the Indian Body-Building, Physique, Figure, Fitness, and Athletic Model community, media personalities, actors, and athletes worldwide. She has appeared on Entertainment Tonight, several television commercials, fitness magazines, radio, and podcasts. Her clients consist of corporations, health practices, and individuals across 10+ countries.

Kim serves on the International teaching staff at Gayo Fitness Academy, Mumbai and Brussels Universities. She's a provider of credentialing certifications and continuing education for the health and fitness industries, offering CME & CEU credits and teaches for the Pro PTA, accepted by NASM, ISSA, ACSM, and NSCA.

Kim has integrated the Healthcare and Fitness Industries by connecting physical activity and functional fitness into the health care system, collaborating with physicians to deliver full and holistic care to patients.

Kim has leveraged her trademarked technology to help transform herself and now thousands of individuals through her exclusive programs over her career.

https://www.thewellnessuniverse.com/world-changers/kim-marie-pauline-ms/activity/

CHAPTER 11

DETOXIFY

DISCOVER AND RELIEVE TOXIC STRESS

by Rosemary Levesque, LSH

MY STORY

OUR PERSONAL TOXIC ENVIRONMENT

The smell of fresh rain on cedar welcomed me home. After living and teaching abroad in industrialized South Korea and Europe for more than six years, the scent drew me into pleasant childhood memories of forests, gardens, and family. My heart conjured dreams of finally settling in, building a home, and starting my own family. Our new home in the Pacific Northwest would be built to our specifications, bringing the best of nature to surround and embrace our dwelling. We imagined a big yard with plenty of grass for the children to run and play. I wanted to plant a garden so I could grow plump tomatoes that we could eat fresh from the vine, or can delicious sauces for winter suppers. Our kids would help me plant peas by poking a short finger in the dirt, careful to place a wrinkled, round seed in the earthy hole, and finally covering each hole with a pat and a small handprint. Squash and pumpkins would trail off the edges to claim their space among the bordering landscape, ensuring successful fall celebrations for Halloween and Thanksgiving.

Planning our home and yard was fun. Our contractors noted the durability of pressure-treated wood used to construct the raised garden beds. Ornamental cherry trees and grafted fruit trees dotted the landscape among pretty ground covers, hybrid roses, and other non-native species. A large deck of pressure-treated wood gained us a view of the Oregon coastal mountain range and yielded space for our barbecue grill, potted flowers, bird feeders, and outdoor seating.

The cedar fence bordering the back yard provided a safe enclosure for the dog and kids. My husband maintained it carefully every year, preserving the wood with an oil stain spray. He cared for the deck similarly, and we knew that the treatment was working as we saw the rainwater bead up, glistening when the sun finally shone. Though the smell was strong, we kept the windows shut for a few days.

Inside our home was like many others. Hardwood floors in the kitchen shined with a lacquer coat, and new vinyl seemed more appropriate for the bathroom and laundry room floors. Our beige wall-to-wall carpeting resisted stains, a big advantage with young children, and messy fingers. New paint for a new home and wallpaper glued to our bedroom walls offered a luxurious look like a picture out of Architectural Digest.

As our new neighborhood filled in, two-story homes lined the streets. Families moved in, complete with kids and pets. The hum of weekly yard maintenance took away tall bags of grass clippings and blew debris into tidy submission. White and green speckled granules dispersed onto the lawn every few weeks promoted an abundance of tall, green comfort between our toes and more clippings every week. Periodic sprays of unknown ingredients guaranteed results to keep weeds and bugs away.

When the strawberry root weevil chewed away at our new, ornamental plants, our yard chemical guy applied more sprays and poisons. **We were like many other families in middle-class America, creating our own space without a clue about the poisonous trap of toxic stress we had set for ourselves. Looking back at that time, I see how I would have done things a lot differently.**

I can't remember when I first became concerned about chemical use in our home and yard. The idea of toxic stress, body burden, and heavy metals stored in my body never really entered my mind. Even as a biologist, I didn't make the connection of personal toxicity to infertility and miscarriage.

However, I did have two successful pregnancies, not without challenges. When my children were young, I began to notice other health issues that I just "lived with." There always seemed to be too much hair in the drain after my shower. My weak fingernails bent and tore easily. A good night's sleep eluded me because I constantly awoke during the night, gasping for air. Daily fatigue turned to concern as I felt myself almost nodding off while driving my daughter to after-school lessons. Allergies to not only grasses and pollen, but apparently to foods too, closed off my throat during meals, as I choked on the smallest morsels. Easily angered, my moods seemed to have a life of their own. This was no way to live and raise my family, but I did. What was the alternative? Drugs? Not for me.

Certain events stand out that contributed to our decision to halt the use of chemicals, insecticides, fertilizers, and herbicides entirely. One of the most memorable and saddest was the loss of my daughter's English budgie, a very sweet, blue bird who entertained us constantly with trills and songs. The fumes from some household chemicals are deadly to birds, a fact we discovered too late. With subsequent birds in our family, we became much more conscientious and learned to be careful since birds are sensitive to many chemicals. Off-gassing from non-stick pans and non-stick surfaces in ovens, common air fresheners like the one seen in commercials to cover terrible odors like a fresh breeze, pesticides, contaminants and molds in packaged bird seed, candles and cleaners all can easily kill a bird.

Acute exposure to obvious toxics is not necessary to experience the effects of toxicity. In our homes and offices, classrooms and gardens, we are the "canaries in the coal mine" or, as in our case, the budgie in the kitchen, vulnerable to the accumulated effects of heavy metals, industrial pollutants, and other toxics. Adult humans living in this self-created toxic world are participants in the experiment. Still, our pets and children, living in a tainted environment, eating processed, packaged foods, and enduring exposure to industrial chemicals directly on their skin, show the results of toxicity at a much greater rate.

Our family adapted to a gradual process of eliminating some toxic practices and incorporating safer alternatives. We stopped using styrofoam cups, wax candles, artificial fragrances of fabric softener, and non-stick pans. We became conscientious about reading food labels and avoiding harmful ingredients. Yet even in my motivation to make positive changes, we all continued to carry a toxic burden accumulated from childhood, tolerating frequent colds that evolved into pneumonia, ear infections, allergies, mood swings, and anxiety.

THE TOOL

THE SOURCE OF TOXICS

"Toxics" (as a noun) is any poisonous substance from either chemical or biological sources, whereas "toxins" are poisons only from biological sources, either plant or animal. We all have both. Humans absorb and accumulate toxics from food, water, air, direct contact, medicines and medical practices, pesticides and fertilizers, the products we buy, and even from the products used to build our homes.

According to the Environmental Protection Agency, the six most common air pollutants are ozone, particulate matter, carbon monoxide, nitrogen oxides, sulfur dioxide, and lead. Ground-level ozone, one of the worst air pollutants, reacts with volatile organic compounds and nitrous oxides from air fresheners, off-gassing from new carpets, glues, and paint and wood finishes, resulting in an increase in formaldehyde (a potent carcinogen), irritating the lungs.

"According to a five-year EPA study, the air in American homes has chemical contamination levels of 70 times greater than the outdoor air. In fact, over 150 chemicals found in the average home actually cause 50 percent of all illnesses and have been linked to allergies, birth defects, cancer, and other abnormalities."

In 1962 Rachel Carson, biologist, environmentalist, and author of *The Silent Spring* shook the world, beginning the environmental movement. Though I was not even a teenager, I remember my older brother showing me this impactful book. Today, I feel that Rachel Carson and I have a little something in common, a voice about the effects of toxicity on all life on earth. DDT, she documented, is a highly toxic pesticide that causes genetic mutations and threatens extinction for many species of birds. DDT persists in the environment and accumulates in greater concentrations up the food chain.

In 1972, ten years following the release of *The Silent Spring* , DDT was banned for use in the United States. Yet even today, DDT and related compounds, PFOAs and PFAs are detected in human breast milk and the umbilical cord blood of newborn babies. Why does this matter?

Toxic Burden Creates Toxic Stress.

Toxic Stress Manifests as Dis-Ease.

THE PRICE OF TOXIC STRESS

For the first time in our history, we witness the birth of a generation with more serious health problems, earlier deaths, higher cancer rates, more heart disease, and familiarity with asthma, greater frequency of autism, and unprecedented obesity than ever before.

The body naturally detoxifies, constantly. What the body can't eliminate, it stores. The liver, for example, emulsifies fats and filters blood coming from the digestive tract. Kidneys clean toxics out of the blood, acting as very efficient filters. The kidneys, miraculous organ-filters located in the middle of the back, clean metabolic waste from the blood. This waste results from normal chemical reactions in the body such as digestion, cell death, response to stress, exercise, and exposure to environmental toxics. Kidneys also help balance the minerals in the body, help regulate pH, and produce hormones that promote the formation of red blood cells in the bone marrow. It may be impossible to completely understand the functions of the liver, kidneys, and other organs as they relate to physical and emotional health. For now, however, we know that these vital, complex, and indispensable organs work hard to protect us.

Unfortunately, unlike the filters that can be changed in your car or home, the kidneys, liver, and other detoxifying organs cannot be swapped out. They must be cleaned or detoxified.

Some toxics (medications, chemicals in food, chemicals in the environment, etc.) are neutralized, metabolized, and eliminated while others, like heavy metals, are stored, hidden away in fat cells, bone marrow, and other tissues to help protect the body from harm.

Yet, lead replaces calcium in the bones (osteoporosis). Mercury replaces oxygen on hemoglobin in red blood cells and interrupts the energy released from mitochondria (chronic fatigue). Mercury also interferes with the formation of the myelin sheath, the protective layer around nerve cells. The short-circuiting nerve cells might appear as muscle spasms, Alzheimer's, Parkinson's, MS, autism, nervousness, depression, or anxiety.

The news is not all bad. I wouldn't leave you without an answer or without hope. The path isn't easy, either. Just as I asked my students throughout the years to be curious, investigate, learn, and share, I ask that you do a few simple things:

- Become aware by looking beyond the obvious
- Find empowerment in knowledge
- Visualize your healthy, productive, and strong future
- Make good choices
- Detoxify

In fact, there's an easy four-step process you can use to shift your energies toward a healthier life and cleaner environment. It's the Four A's; Awareness, Adjustment, Alternatives, and Action.

THE FOUR A'S

AWARENESS

Awareness of toxics in your personal environment develops over time, but the earlier you become aware, the sooner you can make adjustments to your lifestyle, find alternatives and implement natural strategies to reduce stress and the body burden of toxicity. The cost of becoming aware is quite reasonable. Paying attention to news articles, current events, and environmental advocacy organizations such as the Environmental Working

Group, the Washington Toxics Coalition, National Geographic "Our Toxic Homes" interactive guide, and Tox Town from the National Library of Medicine are great resources.

Learn to read between the lines on food labels, advertising, and medical claims (including medicines, vaccines, and other pharmaceuticals). Become familiar with the names of toxic substances so you can recognize them and take steps to avoid them.

ADJUSTMENT

Choosing to reduce toxicity may be the most important adjustment you can ever make. You may have always used the microwave to cook food, drank from Styrofoam cups, or fed your family processed foods. Choosing to eat differently, avoid certain products or practices, and incorporate healthier alternatives may also be done gradually. You'll notice the difference, and adjustments will become second-nature.

ALTERNATIVES

Sometimes finding healthier alternatives is easy, and other times it's just better to let harmful practices go. With greater consumer awareness, manufacturers are developing products that are BPA-free (plastic water bottles and some canned foods), mercury-free (fish oil supplements and some children's vaccines), pesticide-free (organic foods), and antibiotic and hormone-free (meats and dairy products). However, be aware of cool advertising gimmicks that prey upon the consumer. "Natural" comes with guidelines that allow some ingredients to be not natural. Sugar-free or fat-free may have chemical substitutes that have harmful side-effects. BPA-free might have a different chemical that's just as bad, but not yet proven harmful.

ACTION

Information is only as good as the steps you take toward healthier living. You can't really say that you're aware of the issues around plastics and pesticides in foods, and not make better choices to avoid these harmful chemicals and actively detoxify. Throwing up your hands in resignation that the toxicity problem is just "too big" or denying that there's any significance toward impacting your own health just won't serve you in the long run. Take action. Every step counts—moments matter. Choices make a difference. Manufacturers do listen. You can do this.

PRACTICE AWARENESS

Can you find the toxics in your home, school, office, and outdoor environments? Ask for my Guide to Toxics and Personal Toxicity Test. Be a detective in your own home. Uncover the toxics and work to remove them. Find healthier alternatives or make choices to avoid them.

PRACTICE ALTERNATIVES AND ACTION - WHAT YOU CAN DO

Follow this handy guide to help you start to detoxify:

- Actively pursue the safe removal of mercury fillings.
- You need more than a detox bath or detox diet, both of which can cause uncomfortable side-effects as toxins move through your system. Actively detoxify your body daily with an effective mineral oral chelator designed specifically to attract, trap, and eliminate heavy metals. Ask me how.
- Use air purifiers in your home and office. Select ones with a HEPA filter and avoid adding ozone to your indoor air.
- Make sure your vacuum also has a HEPA filter.
- Use water filters on all faucets, even showers. Though reverse osmosis water and distilled water are free of toxics, they also lack life-sustaining minerals. Look for filters that provide both – removing toxics and adding minerals.
- Avoid harsh chemicals such as bleach and furniture polish for cleaning. Try baking soda, vinegar, and "green" products and natural oils for cleaning and freshening.

- Avoid synthetic fragrances and air fresheners, paraffin candles, scented toilet paper, drier sheets, and fabric treatments of any kind. Avoid wearing and using synthetic fabrics like polyester.

- Become aware of clean choices for your home and/or office. Paints, for example, now come in LOW or NO VOC (volatile organic compounds) options.

- Seek natural pest control options such as diatomaceous earth, borax, and essential oils for ants and other crawling insects. Try beer traps for slugs instead of slug bait. Don't spray chemicals on your garden, in your trees, or on the lawn. You can have a healthy, pest-free garden with natural gardening.

- Avoid chemical flea and tick control for your pets. Never apply any chemicals to their skin or yours. Avoid chemical treatments on decking – deadly for dogs.

- Take your shoes off when you come indoors to avoid tracking outside toxics into your home.

- Use a salt lamp to help control molds in the air. Keep moist areas in your home well ventilated. Remove moldy materials and clean moldy areas carefully or hire a professional who follows mold cleaning protocols.

- Replace old bedding or old carpeting, but choose natural materials with no stain-resistant coating and avoid foam rubber.

- New furniture, new carpeting, and new drapes have all been treated with chemicals to resist stains, resist mold and bacteria and resist wrinkles. These are all toxic, so request no additional coating or choose products that are natural and not treated. Never re-treat carpeting with stain-resistant chemicals.

THE RESULTS OF DETOXIFICATION

Once I discovered that stress from toxicity caused dis-ease, my quest for detoxification became the foundation for building a healthy future for myself and my family. There's a direct correlation between detoxification, the achievement of optimal health, and reducing stress.

A friend asked me recently if I could share my best testimony for detoxification. I answered, "The best testimony is the one you never have to tell."

Healthy cells have no toxicity. Healthy blood cells carry oxygen to other cells without fail. Healthy cells of the pancreas produce insulin with great precision to maintain correct blood sugar levels—healthy cells of the brain fire messages flawlessly for us to move and think clearly. Healthy muscle cells perform every muscle action – both voluntary and involuntary – to do everything from heartbeat to that perfect golf swing. Healthy cells of the immune system fight germs and disease with great accuracy and unrelenting strength. In other words, optimal health comes from the body's ability to create new, healthy cells every day. Old or damaged cells are replaced every day.

You can have a new liver, new kidneys, new, solid bones, a clearer mind, and less stress when you detoxify daily – now and forever. Ultimately, the freedom from toxicity you experience manifests energetically and physically as the expansion of your Highest Potential.

Be the highest version of YOU without toxic stress.

Prevention is better than cure. Daily practice through awareness and implementation goes a long way toward relieving toxic stress and healing. It's my greatest hope that these words resonate with you.

Owner and founder of Second Nature Healing®, Rosemary offers real solutions for personal detoxification and optimal healing. She helps set the standard for Spiritual Growth for Lightworkers and offers in-person and online courses for Lightworkers on their journey. Throughout the years of working with detoxification, energy, animal guides, nature, and healing, Rosemary brings to life ancient wisdom for the modern world. She incorporates Shamanic practices in her intuitive Sound and Reiki classes and healing sessions as well as her life's work to remind us how to BE in the world, to heal old wounds in our Akashic records, and access the power within All That Is.

Rosemary Levesque was born in Hawaii and feels like she brought the energy of the islands into her work from the moment she was born. Trained as a Biology teacher, Rosemary taught in public and private schools around the world until she paused to raise her family in Portland, OR.

As a natural teacher, mentor, and psychic intuitive, Rosemary helps to awaken the healer within you to incorporate healing wisdom for stress release and personal growth into your life. https://www.thewellnessuniverse. com/world-changers/rosemarylevesque/

Licensed Spiritual Healer

Reiki Master

Shaman, Certified Vibrational Sound Master Teacher

CHAPTER 12

DE-CLUTTER YOUR MIND

ENHANCE PRODUCTIVITY WITHOUT THE BURNOUT

by Dr. Toni Warner-McIntyre, LCSW, MEd, MSW

MY STORY

I looked like an outward success while feeling like an inward mess for as long as I could remember. To make matters worse, I was in denial about both.

It was a nice spring day; I was standing in my dorm room, my typical emotional armor was still on, yet it felt like I was busting from its encasement from the inside out.

At the ripe old age of 20, I had long been a pro at setting my mind to something, staying focused, and getting through, without complaint or pause for my feelings or needs. I was an achiever. I was a doer—a headstrong, multi-tasking, autonomous woman.

I wore that description with pride, but I hid the immense pressure that boiled beneath it.

This particular day, the steam from that internal pressure cooker was trying to seep out. It was so thick and compressed from all the years of avoidance.

I tried to resist.

I paced back and forth. I sat on my bed. I looked at the scissors and then looked away. I saw the pill bottle and averted my eyes. I tried to hold myself inside my all-familiar, invisible protective casing, but I couldn't. I felt like I was busting open at the seams as tears began to slide down my face.

Even as a sophomore in college, I'd accomplished a lot. I rarely ever asked anyone for anything, so as not to be a burden. I was always volunteering to do what I could. I was a residential assistant and had gone above and beyond to create a fun, supportive atmosphere for my rooms of ambitious female engineers. I was up for a bunch of awards as a result. I thought I'd done everything I could to be the best possible me; to show I could be successful; to show I wasn't a stereotype; to prove I could be of value.

A's, Honors, AP, Gifted.

Extra-curriculars.

Leadership positions.

People-pleasing and appeasing.

Asking, *"How can I help?"* while withholding any expression of my own needs, for fear of judgment, rejection, or feeling vulnerable.

I craved the acceptance that action and achievement brought me. It made me feel like I was doing something of purpose. I was terrified of living a purposeless life. I needed to help. I needed to do. I needed to give. I needed to do well. I needed to stay strong and be independent.

Vulnerability was a weakness; I couldn't be weak. I felt like I'd learned that lesson straight out of the womb.

Be good Toni. Don't want more than you have. Don't ask, just give. Don't be too emotional. Don't be too loud. Don't be too difficult. Don't be too needy. Do what you have to. Work hard. Achieve. Be successful. Help others.

The endless litany of requirements to be deemed good enough, played in the background of my mind incessantly. It never felt like a choice. I worked tirelessly because I thought I had to.

CONTROL

Control. I felt I had none of it, so I constantly grasped for it. If I got good grades, I could control the praise I got from adults. If I stayed neutral,

I could control being the middle-peg between my parents during their divorce. If I kept my emotions to myself and just focused on doing well in school and being there for other people, then I could control the possibility of being rejected or judged.

Except the more I fought for control, the less in control I felt; the more I wondered what I was doing wrong, what I needed to do more of.

Is there something wrong with me?

So much of my life felt beyond my control; constant issues with weight, never really feeling seen or heard by my family (or really anyone), the emotional backlash of the divorce, always seeming like people were trying to categorize me into boxes that I never fit into.

Not black enough. Not really white.

What am I? Do I even belong here?

On this particular spring evening, the build-up sprung a leak. I lost my grip on any semblance of control that I thought I had. Like a heavy, wet, and weighted blanket, the hopelessness and unworthiness enveloped me. Somehow, the scissors were now in my hand, and a handful of pills were already down my throat. My mind wasn't racing so much anymore, though. It was focused on one thing now.

God, this is your chance to show me. I firmly spoke in my mind. *If I still have purpose to fulfill, show me. If I don't, let me know. Please.*

I desperately needed to know.

For a moment, I felt relief. I'd finally done something that would show me, for sure, if I had more purpose to fulfill. I'd finally know if that deeply hidden belief that I was meant for big things was actually real, or if it was all just made up in my head.

I'd finally get the answers I'd been seeking: *Am I worthy? Am I the good kind of different? Should I be alive? Is there still more for me to do? Do I belong here?*

That relief lasted only a moment, as I came back into my physical reality and realized that I needed to stop trying to be so damn independent all the time and finally ask for help.

Sobbing, I called "Stephanie. I need you." She rushed over and drove me to the hospital. Laying on that hospital bed, white-gowned, black charcoal in my stomach to rid the toxins; I remember looking at my mom's face. I wondered what she was thinking, but I didn't dare ask.

Awkward silence. Doctor talking. Me, still feeling unseen, unheard, and completely misunderstood.

They called it attempted suicide. I called it a pleading for guidance, a last-ditch effort to verify that I indeed have more purpose to fulfill in this life.

I was forced to stay on the psychiatric ward for about 10 days. No one listened to me. A grown man attempted to force himself into my room and onto me. It was my roommate who protected me. My experience was so bad that part of me just tried to forget about it.

After an un-encouraging talk with the psychiatric doctor, I was released.

When I rejoined the public, things were different. I lost my residential assistant position. They redistributed the awards I was lined up for and gave them to others. I had to leave my fellow RA's and residents without any real explanation. I was mandated to counseling if I wanted to continue with the traveling abroad opportunities I had already lined up.

It felt like all the action I had taken, all the work and effort I had put in to be enough, to be better, it was all for naught. I'd tried to do my best, give my best, and be my best, but it felt like it didn't matter anymore. It felt like the fruits of that labor were taken away, or were threatened to be.

I was no longer feeling hopeless. I was feeling angry. At the time, I didn't realize that was actually emotional progress.

I guess part of me did die that day. I left those experiences with a different outlook on my life. I wasn't feeling hopeless anymore, but I did feel a renewed sense of purpose.

For the most part, no one knew I was dealing with anxiety and depression. If I'm honest, I guess I didn't know that either. I'd felt so misplaced, like I didn't "fit in" or belong, for so long, that the anxiety and depression experience had just become my "familiar."

Along the beginning stages of my life journey, what I had learned is that if I just worked hard to please others, accomplish goals, or exceed expectations, people were generally pleased with me. They liked me or acknowledged me in some positive fashion, even if only momentarily or situationally.

That felt good.

It was reinforcing, but that feeling never lasted long. I always had to work for more.

The more action I took, the more success I'd show, the more I'd momentarily felt I belonged.

Action had become my drug of choice, and I didn't even know it.

I've since discovered that many high achievers, leaders, and compassionate-yet-independent folks, tend to hide their emotional challenges pretty well, too. So, even though I thought I was alone then, I now realize I'm not the only one who suffered in this way. There are many amazing people out there who are looking like an outward success and feeling like an inward mess, suffering silently inside.

I never questioned my life having purpose after that life-altering experience during my sophomore year of college. I brought life into this world the following year, and became the mom of a heart-warming little girl; my daughter, Jadeyn. She brought an even more powerful purpose to my life. She reminded me of how precious life is, and how powerful we as humans are. We have the power to create, nurture, and to mold our lives.

I was determined; I was going to use my power for good.

I didn't pause long, though. My daughter was by my side in classes at a week old. I pumped on the bathroom floor at the University. I went straight into getting my first Master's degree as soon as I graduated with my Bachelor's. She was on my hip the day of graduation, as I walked across that stage to receive my hard-earned diploma.

I didn't realize it at the time, but looking back, that spring day marked the beginning of a new era for me. Having my daughter the following year was a clear indicator of the significance of that new era.

Despite my renewed sense of purpose and my dedication to crafting a supportive and loving life for my daughter, it took several more years and a few bouts of burnout before I learned how addicted to action I had become.

The pains of my past had been harnessing the reigns of my future for far too long.

I believed that since I had on my emotional armor, was focused on achievement, taking tons of action, and being super independent, then I was taking control of my life. I thought all of this meant I wasn't playing a victim role. I didn't want to resonate with feeling like a victim of anything or anyone, because it led me back to that place of feeling powerless.

I refused to feel powerless.

Yet, I had let my goals and the voracity of my constant need to "do" define me.

There were plenty of signs that I was feeling out of control and overwhelmed, but I ignored them. I told myself that I could tolerate more and more stress, therefore welcoming more and more stress.

Others may need help, and I'll be glad to help them, lead them, and support them, but I'm good. I've got this. I still don't want to burden anyone.

I was the exception. I always found a way to justify constant goal setting, endless action, and lack of self-care.

Helping others helped me distract from helping myself.

Staying busy kept me from dealing with the underlying emotions and fears that I didn't know how (or that I had) to address.

I thought that over-time it would all sort itself out. I'd hoped it'd go away or not affect me or my relationships. I could work hard and rise above. I believed I had dealt with what needed to be dealt with and could escape having to deal with the rest, but it just compounded itself.

That's what happens, you know? No matter how many goals you accomplish. No matter how much money you make. No matter how successful you are, what you look like, or how much you help others, if you ignore your own feelings, don't tend to your own needs, or think like you have to prove that you belong, it's going to hurt you. It's going to build up. It's going to show up in your life in some way.

For most busy, ambitious folks, there is a mental clutter, an overwhelm that takes hold. It's frustrating and can feel debilitating. Action seems like an ideal distraction. It feels productive until it's not anymore; until the over-action results in disconnection, self-doubt, self-sabotage, exhaustion, or some other undesired consequence of chronically operating in "on" mode.

The real irony here is that the more we over-work ourselves, criticize ourselves, ignore our emotions, and refuse to slow down, the less productive we become. Seriously, research supports this. Our brains can't function optimally when thwarting the communication process between the brain and body by cutting off our emotions. We can't operate when we haven't taken the time to maintain and tend to our own internal systems properly. We don't have as much to give when we are on "E" all the time. That's why the mental clutter is building up. That's why good people and strong leaders burn out.

That's what I had to learn to do differently, and when I did, I felt free.

That's also why today, I want to share a two-part tool that helps with reducing the mental clutter, thereby enhancing our ability to step in, gain clarity, feel better, reduce burnout and boost productivity (among many other desirable benefits).

You can find a video-walk-thru of the following exercise here: https://www.thewellnessuniverse.com/world-changers/toniwarner/

THE TOOL

PART ONE: VERGENCE

Vergence is a tool that uses the power of the brain and body connection to help calm the nervous system and promote inward soothing. I learned about Vergence through my training in Brainspotting, which is an incredibly powerful method I use with clients. Brainspotting helps my clients and me to tap into the mid-part of the brain, which is largely responsible for processing emotions. Although Brainspotting requires a trained professional, you can use Vergence on your own, from the comfort of your home, office chair, or wherever you may be when you're in need of easing the overwhelm that often accompanies mind clutter.

The process is simple. It may seem too simple—no need to over-complicate this process. The power of this process lies in your full attention to it. The more you practice it, the better it can serve you.

Use your finger or a pen/pencil and put it upright in front of your eye-line, about 8-12 inches out in front of your face.

Gaze straight at your fingertip/object for about 5-8 seconds. Take deep breaths in through your nose and slowly out of your mouth as you gaze.

Now, shift your gaze beyond your fingertip/object. Allow your eyes to look past your finger to the wall/area about six or so feet beyond it. Gaze there for 5-8 seconds, while taking deep breaths in through your nose and slowly out of your mouth.

Bring your eyes back to your fingertip/object and repeat this process for 2-6 minutes, or until you're feeling less overwhelmed (whichever comes first).

Notice how you feel. Take notice of any shifts in your feeling state or in your body. It's okay if you yawn or experience some other bodily reaction during this process; that is your nervous system calming.

If it is helpful, you may think of your vision as narrowing and then expanding throughout this process.

Now, this next part of the process is not required, but I have found it to be incredibly powerful for both myself and my clients, so I highly suggest you give it a try a few times before deciding whether or not you include it in your own practice. For this part of the process, you'll need a piece of paper and something to write with.

PART TWO: CONTROL CHECK-IN

Draw two separate circles on a sheet of paper.

Label one circle "in control" and the other "out of control."

Thinking about the current challenge on your mind, write in the "out of control" circle what's outside of your control about the situation.

In the "in control" circle, write what's within your control.

Review your circles and consciously choose which one you'll focus on as you move forward.

That's it! Two parts and ten steps. Now, notice how much calmer and less stressed you feel. Are you able to think more clearly? Has the mind clutter begun to lift, or perhaps cleared up a ton? Notice what you've experienced here, and without judgment, allow whatever shift has happened for you to be okay. The more you practice this, the more the benefits will become amplified.

It's important to remember that this type of mental work is most powerful when it becomes a practice with multiple components. I've started you off in this chapter with a simple, foundational tool you can use along your journey. This tool can help you calm your nervous system in times of overwhelm. There are more layers and levels to a long-term, life-enhancing practice, which has taken me years to learn. I will always continue to expand my practices and to help myself grow. If you're interested in learning and mastering a broader scale practice, I invite you to visit my resource link to explore those next steps.

Dr. Toni is a licensed psychotherapist in the state of PA, mom of 3, former behavior specialist, and Life Advisor for the Busy & Ambitious. For more than a decade, she has been a parenting professional, working and studying in the fields of human behavior, psychology, and sexuality.

Having navigated her own mental health issues and relationship challenges, she knows what it's like to wrestle with the relentless need to achieve and overly active mind clutter. She didn't just learn how to both prevent and exit burnout through her professional work and academic studies- she personally traversed the turmoil of burnout herself. She's experienced the process of stepping out of burnout without compromising herself, her success, her health or her relationships.

Dr. Toni leverages her knowledge and experience gained both personally and professionally, and combines it with the most current research and brain science. This combination allows her to combine both practical steps and tools with the power of the mind, providing unprecedented support to her coaching clients.

Dr. Toni earned her Masters degree in Clinical Social Work, her Masters degree in Education and her Doctorate of Philosophy in Human Sexuality at Widener University. She's completed numerous certification programs, earning a robust amount of experience in areas such as coaching, trauma, mindfulness and various elements of human behavior and psychology.

Dr. Toni is the founder of Dr. Toni Coaches, LLC, a coaching, educating and consulting business. It's mission is to inspire and enact meaningful change in the world by helping impact makers create work, life & relationship balance, allowing them to more deeply and meaningfully live, love, connect and share their gifts, enhancing their lives and the lives of others.

Dr. Toni is also the founder of Authentically Me Psychotherapy, LLC, where she supports high achieving and creative individuals who are struggling with anxiety, depression, trauma, burn out and/or disconnection, to get in touch with their core selves so they can live more fully and authentically aligned lives.

Over the years, she's guided countless people along their life journey, through life transitions, chronic stress, post-trauma, leadership and relationships challenges and more. She's helped them to create a foundation for a less stressful, more fulfilling life that they enjoy living in. When she's not supporting clients, she's laughing with her children, taking nature walks, or enjoying some good old music, dancing or baking (okay, maybe a piece of chocolate and espresso, too).

To connect with Dr. Toni further, and access her video walk-thru of the above tools, visit: http://www.thewellnessuniverse.com/world-changers/toniwarner/

*** Disclaimer: This does not serve as medical advice or treatment. Talk with your doctor if there are potential conditions or concerns that may be impacted by this activity. Please note that coaching and therapy are not one in the same; they are separate services, and the above mentioned are separate business entities. If you are unsure which service best fits your needs, simply reach out and ask: mail@authenticallymepsychotherapy.com or hello@drtonicoaches.com

CHAPTER 13

PAUSE WITH PURPOSE

TAME THE CHAOS AND
RESET THE NERVOUS SYSTEM

by Jennifer Wren Tolo, RN, MA, CRM, CPT

MY STORY

I was a critical care nurse, married to a surgeon, whose life course pivoted when my second son had a massive neonatal stroke and my third son had leukemia.

I woke up terrified after the birth of my second son.

"Where's my baby?"

He'd been sent to a children's hospital 30 miles away after a massive stroke, seizing. Other people's babies were crying all around me, and all I wanted was to hold my son. This was not at all like I expected and not at all like when my first son was born. I was so confused and overwhelmed with my head spinning from people talking at me and all the unanswered questions.

Then I heard a voice inside me say, *"just breathe."*

Once I did, the fog lifted. I knew that I just needed to be with my son, connect and tune in, and he would help me know what was needed. I had to recover from what I expected the birth of my son to be and allow what was to unfold and reveal my path.

I had no choice but to turn to the voice of my intuition for a way to heal my son. I became an Integrative Health Coach and Educator, an ACE Certified Personal Trainer, Certified Karuna Reiki Master, and Certified Mindfulness Practitioner and Educator.

My third son was diagnosed with high-risk acute lymphoblastic leukemia on the very day I found out the baby I was carrying was my fourth boy. This time, I had the tools and I knew how to trust myself to help my son navigate his cancer treatments and get well.

My own health suffered from putting out so many fires and worrying about the kids. I was a warrior mom, constantly prepping for battle, stuck in fight or flight, exhausted and depleted.

I had migraines. I wasn't sleeping well. My metabolism was so out of whack that I couldn't lose weight despite diet and exercise. My husband got melanoma and my immune system was so depressed that I came down with the shingles.

I remember sitting in my living room, baby asleep in the infant swing, reading to my 3-year-old and 5-year-old while my 7-year-old was in school. I was seeing pixels on the page, dropping my speech as my right arm felt numb. I called my husband at work as I wasn't sure what was wrong.

"Call 9-1-1, I think you may be having a stroke!" he said.

"I can't call 9-1-1! Who is going to take care of the kids? I'll be alright."

After my husband, stuck 200 miles away at a Shriner's hospital, begged me to go to the hospital, I agreed and called a friend to come watch the kids while I drove myself to the hospital. It turned out to be an atypical migraine.

This experience woke me up to the need to put myself on the "take care of" list. I finally realized that I had to put my oxygen mask on first before I could be there for my family. I needed to deal with the emotions and stress of my busy life before I burned out completely.

The good news is, my boys and I are all healthy and strong. We still have our challenges and obstacles, but we have learned to adjust, reset and grow one day, one empowered moment at a time. I healed myself from chronic fatigue, depression, gastrointestinal problems, and migraines.

Once I started to pick my head up from the frenzy of my life and dust myself off, I realized I can't be there for my kids until I take care of myself first. I found I couldn't listen to my intuition while I was running myself into the ground.

I learned to take pauses, or mindful moments, throughout my day to calm the chaos of my life and reset my nervous system. I realized time was a created thing and, I needed to create time, even just two minutes, to pause with the purpose of resetting my "fight or flight," finding calm in the chaos and tuning into the answers, the wisdom of my mind, body and spirit so I could take back control of my health and happiness.

THE TOOL

I believe self-care is one of the best forms of health care out there. It is preventative medicine. When we can stop, and be in the present moment and connect to our body, mind and spirit needs, we can tap into our greatest wisdom and power.

One of the tools and techniques I like to teach as a foundational self-care practice is the power of the pause to reset the nervous system and take back control over the mind and body. When we take a moment, and tune into the mind and body starting with slow deep breaths, we can calm the nervous system, clear the 'fight or flight' and tune into to the messages of our body, mind and spirit. Science has shown that as little as two minutes of deep breathing can reset the nervous system by activating the "relaxation response."

We often get caught up in the spin, the reaction to emotional triggers, stress, and the barrage of thoughts flooding our mind in any given moment. This can bring us out of the present moment, trigger anxiety and disconnect us from our rational thought and power we possess when we are calm and in the present moment.

This energetic, emotional, and hormonal 'spin' can cause us to be reactive instead of responsive to our environment and our loved ones, clients or coworkers. It keeps us in the "fight or flight," sympathetic nervous system feedback loop. Our energy impacts the energy around us. When we can calm the chaos in our body and mind, balancing our own energy and emotions, we can calm and balance the energy around us.

Many people say they do not have time to practice self-care. What they do not realize is pausing with purpose and taking mindful moments can reset the nervous system and anchor us in the present moment. All it takes is a few minutes to reset the nervous system, which is why I call these mindful moments. Then, you can tame the chaos in the mind and body and take back control of your health and happiness, one choice, one thought and one conscious action at a time.

Stress is an inevitable part of our lives. The common theme in the constant doing, constant distraction and drive of life is the challenge to reset and relax. This is the stress of life and the biggest disruptor to balance, health and happiness. This continual motion, overthinking and future focus is throwing the nervous system out of balance, keeping us in the fight or flight mode with little time to rest and digest. It is no wonder we have so many chronic health complaints, including anxiety and depression.

Gastrointestinal problems are one of the most common concerns bringing people to seek medical advice. When the body is exposed to chronic stress, or a state of sympathetic nervous system overload, it disrupts digestion, sleep, brain function, hormone function, immune function, and feeds inflammation in the body.

Here is the good news; you CAN take back control over your health and your happiness by learning to be more present in your life and manage the inevitable stressors of life. The first step is to pause with the purpose of resetting the nervous system and tuning into the messages of the body, mind and spirit. Only when we are aware of what is going on in our mind, body and environment and how we are reacting can we take back control and purposefully create change. When we are future focused, we often miss out on the here and now, which is the only place we have control over our choices, thoughts and actions.

When are times you may need to take a *Pause* with the purpose of resetting your nervous system?

- Before you eat a meal so you can better "rest and digest" and tap into the parasympathetic nervous system.

- When you are in traffic, maybe with muscles tense, worried about being late or even when you are having a bit of "road rage."

- When you feel overwhelmed and/or are have trouble focusing.

- When you feel anxious, angry, worried, afraid, overly emotional.

- When someone says, or does something and you are about to react from an emotional place or you feel "triggered."

- When you transition from home to work and work to home and need to "shift gears."

- When you have a food or beverage craving like sugar or caffeine from stress demands on body. In chronic stress, your body looks for energy and adrenaline, hence, sugar and caffeine cravings.

- When you want control, but do not have control or feel powerless.

What we need is to start to calm the chaos, realize that we can only control ourselves and no one else. Change begins within each of us, one moment of awareness, one choice and one action at a time. This is how we begin to tame the chaos of our lives. This is functional self-care and even survival in our chaotic and challenging lives.

Life is full of stress with continuous ups and downs. It is like a roller coaster ride. Sometimes you feel you can handle the ride and throw your hands up laughing, and sometimes your stomach drops and you want to get off the ride and throw up. By recognizing when we need to pause and reset, we can learn to become more stress resilient and feel empowered by our awareness of mind, body and spirit messages and needs as well as by our choices when we are in the present moment.

Here are some *Pause with Purpose* tips and tools:

- Take 4-5 slow, deep, purposeful breaths.

- Tune into the breath and how your body feels, noticing areas of tension, discomfort or sensation.

- With each exhale, consciously release tension in muscles.

- Notice any thoughts and emotions without attaching to or judging them. Just notice them.

- If angry, worried or disappointed, picture a balloon and call the thought and emotion into your mind. With each exhale, blow the thought into the balloon. Notice the balloon fill in your mind's eye.

- Make a choice: Let the balloon and thoughts go, or hold onto them.

- Move your arms up overhead with inhale and quickly lower them with a forceful exhale. Connect breath and movement. Inhalation brings in energy and exhale releases. What do you need in the moment?

- Change your environment by stepping outside, turning your face to the sun, feel the heat on your face and take five deep breaths.

- Practice stating a mantra to shift your mindset and focus on the good vs. bad or to remind yourself that you are safe and in control of yourself.

You do not have to utilize each of these tips or tools. Start with the breath, tune into the body and mind and what you need, what might help you in the moment. Sometimes you need more than the breath, so these are tools to keep in your "Mindful Moment Toolbox" to use as needed.

Stressors are a part of daily life and our body is built to withstand them in acute situations and recover, normalizing our body, maintaining balance. Chronic stress is what can be damaging to our health and happiness as it exhausts our bodies internal resources that help us recover and normalizes. Self-care practices such as meditation, yoga, exercise, massage, hot baths, journaling, and listening or playing music are all ways to help the mind, body and spirit find balance and normalize in our stressful lives.

We do not always have the luxury of time and space to practice lengthy or ritualistic self-care practices, but our body and mind are in desperate need of a reset, particularly when we are stuck in a "fight or flight" feedback loop. This is where the *Pause with Purpose* or mindful moment comes in. You can stop, breathe and tune in to the present moment and check in with your mind, body and spirit for a few minutes anywhere, anytime.

We cannot always control the stressors in our life, but we can control how we react and adapt as well as our choices, decisions regarding self-care, environment and how we treat our body, mind and spirit. A balanced body and nervous system can adapt and recover with more ease and without long term damage.

Recognizing moments when you feel stress or any strong emotion bringing you out of balance is the first step to taking back control of your health and happiness. With awareness, you can recognize the need to reset the nervous system and take a pause to be present, connect to your mind, body and spirit messages and needs. This is where you can be empowered and use the pause with purpose tools to tame the chaos of your life one breath, one action, one thought, one conscious choice at a time.

Self-Care and self-awareness practices are crucial to taming the chaos of life. However, before you can access the higher self and the rational mind, you need to reset and calm the nervous system.

Jennifer Wren Tolo, RN, MA, CRM, CPT is the owner of Butterfly Family Wellness. She is a Whole Health Educator™ and Patient Advocate, Certified Karuna Reiki Master, Integrative Nutritionist, Certified Mindfulness Educator and Certified Personal Trainer. Jen is 'An Integrative Bridge to Health' helping bridge the gaps between modern medical healthcare and alternative healing, between self-care and caring for others, between science and intuition, between illness and wellness and between adults and children. She helps women and children tame the chaos of their lives so they can take back control of their health and happiness one choice, one thought, one action and one reaction at a time.

For more information and to connect with Jennifer, please visit http://www.thewellnessuniverse.com/world-changer/jennifer-tolo/

CHAPTER 14

TAP AND RANT

RELEASE BLOCKED ENERGY FOR EMPOWERED CLARITY

by Carolyn McGee, Intuitive Strategist and Coach

MY STORY

I was beyond frustrated! I had invested thousands of dollars in a high-end marketing program and I could not fully engage in it. I felt as if I kept bumping into a glass wall of personal resistance. The harder I tried to do the work, the greater the resistance I felt. I was beating myself up daily. *I can't believe you are wasting all that money. You never finish anything you start. You are such a loser. You should get a job. You will never be successful as a coach.* I felt like a failure.

As always, the universe truly does have our backs and will repeatedly give us lessons to learn and opportunities to grow and clear the patterns that keep us stuck. A friend invited me to attend a conference, and without even really knowing what I was signing up for, I agreed to go. It was an Emotional Freedom Technique (EFT), also known as tapping conference.

Tapping was a healing tool that I was trained in during my Life Coach Certification. It was a tool that didn't feel right or intuitive to me. I didn't get it. I had huge resistance to using it for myself and my clients. Using tapping caused me stress because I felt like I was walking against the tide, and it drained so much of my energy just getting started with it.

I also struggled with the formality of the way I was trained. Traditional EFT uses a setup phrase *Even though I (fill in your issue), I deeply and completely love and accept myself.* Starting with this statement never felt right to me; it felt counterintuitive to releasing the stored energy. The image of putting a band-aid on a wound, tearing it off, and then leaving the wound raw and open came to mind.

Even with my lack of faith using EFT, I felt compelled to sign up for the program.

It was supposed to help me fully launch my life coaching business. I already had a successful pet care business and had done a lot of self-development work, so I knew that the negative self-talk wasn't true. And yet, it still ran through my mind and slowed my progress.

I found that I could follow along in the training calls with the tapping, but I could not do it on my own. The harder I tried, the more difficult it became. I found myself shutting down and not wanting to engage in this expensive program I signed up for. Committing to this program was my attempt to find a way to move stuck energy, but the opposite was happening.

My education is in engineering management, and I worked 20-plus years in high tech manufacturing. I defaulted back to my analysis background to "figure out" what was blocking me. I made lists and analyzed emotions in an attempt to think my way out of my feelings.

As I made my lists, a pattern rose to the surface. Every place I felt blocked or stuck had something to do with tapping. **This was big!**

Once I realized the problem, I reached out to ask for help. This alone was a big and healing step for me. I felt my energy shift just by asking for support. Two people agreed to tap with me regularly until I could move through the resistance. As a coach, I know the bigger the resistance to something, the higher the need for it is.

These two amazing women had radically different styles of tapping. By opening myself up and being vulnerable about my challenge, I experienced different ways to use this modality for healing. Tapping with Jacqueline allowed me to see the script's value to move certain types of stuck energy.

My engineer could see the value in this process. Lorraine gave me the gift of creatively approaching EFT using my own energy to make it work for me.

We tapped on my resistance to tapping, and I felt the release of trapped energy. As I experienced the healing and energy shifts in my body, it became easier to tap on my own and be more aware of what worked, or not, using the two styles.

What I learned was that there was negativity around following the rules and doing it correctly. I got so wrapped up in doing the process that I couldn't feel my intuition guiding me in what to say. I wanted so badly to do it right that I was tense and not allowing the healing release.

Once the resistance to tapping lessened, I could feel that the setup phrase was not aligned with my energy and healing style. Giving myself the gift of skipping that part of the process opened many possibilities and allowed me to give myself permission to follow my intuition and guidance while tapping.

Each time I tapped, I could feel the release in my body more deeply that allowed the healing energy to integrate. I felt more alive than I ever had. My intuition became even clearer. The next right step became easy to see, and I had the confidence to take the inspired actions to make my coaching business a success.

Tapping became my favorite healing modality. I discovered that I could fully release my resistance to following a script and embrace my intuitive nature. I knew when a script was optimal and when to follow my guidance. Even though I am highly logical and analytical, the intuitive piece of knowing what energy was stuck was a gift that I could offer to myself and my clients.

One day when I was tapping, and the energy felt harder to move, I started to pace around my living room while I tapped. It came to me that movement always helped mental clarity and energy flow for me.

This version of tapping, which I call *Tap and Rant*, was incredibly powerful for my clients and me as it helped move energy in a way that the traditional tapping did not. It was as if I was tricking my body and my clients' bodies into accepting the tapping without letting logic or resistance arise and get in the way. This allowed diving deeper into the issues that were blocked, providing for powerful releases and shifts in peoples' energy away from the negative and into more healing and empowered awareness based on their true intuitive nature.

I continue to offer the *Tap and Rant* method to my clients today, and I use it as part of my personal practices. To me, this approach allows for a more intuitive flow of the intention of the practice. I hope you also find it to be an empowering and effective tool.

THE TOOL

HOW EFT WORKS

Emotional Freedom Technique (EFT), also known as tapping, is the release of trapped energy in our physical bodies. When we experience trauma or a negative emotion, the vibration of that event is stored in our physical body. Unless we consciously release that stored vibration, it blocks the flow of energy in our body. This can cause illness, pain, and lack of energy. We can feel disorientated, experience a lack of motivation to complete tasks, or feel disconnected from life.

Tapping opens the energy circuits of your meridians to clear any trapped energy. When we don't fully feel or process an emotion, the emotion gets stuck and blocks the flow. EFT brings those stuck emotions to the surface, allowing them to be healed and released.

Traditional EFT was first introduced by Gary Craig in 1995. The technique is based on tapping with your fingers on certain points associated with the Chinese meridian system. The meridian system is a circuit of energy points in the physical body associated with our organs and emotions. When these energy points are open, energy flows easily and cleanly in our bodies. When we don't fully process an experience, the points become blocked. Imagine this meridian system as blood vessels for your energy with narrowing of the flow with each negative experience.

Traditional EFT uses a setup phrase to frame the release that we are intending. *"Even though I (fill in your issue), I deeply and completely love and accept myself."* This is tapped on the karate chop point on the side of the hand.

Although the traditional method might work for some, I have found the most effective method for my clients and me is what I call *Tap and Rant* The process goes as follows:

TAP AND RANT

The key to this process is combining freeform thoughts, tapping, and movement.

1. Think of something that bothers you.

2. Then, start to pace somewhere safe (according to Google, pacing means to walk at a steady and consistent speed, especially back and forth and as an expression of one's anxiety or annoyance.)

3. Do a stream of consciousness saying anything that comes into your mind out loud as you tap through the points described below.

   - In between the eyes at the eyebrow
   - The side of each eye on the temple
   - Under the eyes
   - Under the nose
   - On the chin
   - Just below your collarbone
   - Under your arms
   - The top of the head

Please note that the *Tap and Rant* method does not require that one also employ the "karate chop point" to be effective. Suppose one finds this place to help release the energy. In that case, I recommend it is done without using the statement used with the traditional process and instead focusing on the ranting process I have developed.

For this stress releasing method to be effective, you don't have to hit each point precisely. Tap each point 5-7 times and move on to the next point. If you feel like you need to stay on one point longer, then follow your intuition.

The power of this exercise is in moving the energy and getting into a flow. It is the combination of the movement in our bodies with the tapping on the meridian points and the vocalization of what is causing you the stress that quickly releases the trapped energy.

Tapping can feel counterintuitive when first starting. The goal is to amplify the negative emotion so that it can be released. You want to fully feel the emotion as you are tapping so that it is completely removed. You do not need to fear that you are attracting more negativity as it is being released from your body.

STRESS RELEASE TAPPING EXAMPLE

- I am so stressed out
- I don't believe that the universe is conspiring in my favor
- Everything is stacked against me
- Nothing is going my way
- I am so stressed out
- Nothing is working out for me
- Life is so incredibly difficult
- I cannot believe how challenging life is
- I have no one who supports me
- I am all alone
- I have to do everything myself
- Everything I touch is falling apart
- Nothing is easy
- Life is stressful

You want to verbalize the old thought pattern, that unconscious tape in your mind that is negative. This is what you want to speak out loud. It may sound awkward to verbalize what we have termed a negative thought, but those are the subconscious thought patterns running through our body and our energy system all the time. By speaking them out loud, by raising that fight or flight response in our bodies as we tap on these meridian points, we are releasing the energetic charge that has been trapped in our body for sometimes decades.

I like to use both hands and tap on both sides at the same time to amplify the energy release. As you are doing this freeform consciousness tapping, you may remember certain events from your life, or certain memories may come up. When this occurs, follow the energy, speak it out loud and allow it all to be released. As emotions and feelings come up, incorporate those into your rant.

You will know when the cycle is complete when you experience a shift in energy. This may be a yawn, burp, chills, flushing on your skin, or a shudder. As you practice, you will recognize when you release and feel more peace.

Please note that there is no right way, and there is no wrong way to move through this process and vocalize what is coming up. There is only energy to be moved, and using the *Tap and Rant* method is an approach that I have found that enables this to happen effectively and rapidly.

As you are the best advocate for you and your journey, you will know how the *Tap and Rant* method will best serve you. You will be able to have your inner intuition guide you to the way you employ this method. The more you practice this modality, the more energy you will have, and the clearer your thoughts and intuitive connection will be.

Like me, you may benefit from the support of a coach or guide to help you through the process. If so, and you would like my assistance and support, please feel free to reach out to me.

Intuitive Strategist, Coach & Teacher, Carolyn McGee specializes in Amplifying YOUR Intuitive Superpower to listen to, trust, and follow your soul's path to living the most joyful, healthy, connected, abundant, and purposeful life. She has taught thousands of professional, corporate, and entrepreneurial women to trust themselves and their intuition so they can show up in their full power in business and life.

By showing you the way back to your intuition, she helps you enhance your ability to receive messages and understand your guidance 24/7. This empowers you to take inspired action so that you release second-guessing for good, and you feel 100% confident in making crystal clear decisions.

With a background of 20+ years in High Tech, Carolyn knows firsthand the importance of living from a blend of her masculine and feminine energies. Her unique combination of Angel, Animal & Intuitive connection, EFT, Energy Healing, and Ministry created her "Soul Clarity System" for powerful healing, heart-centered connection, and inspired action.

She has co-authored nine bestselling books, is a popular TV co-host and sought-after speaker and blogger. To learn more about Carolyn, or to contact her, visit

https://www.thewellnessuniverse.com/world-changers/carolynmcgee/

CHAPTER 15

DIVINE POWER

INTEGRATING ANGEL ENERGY TO RELEASE LIFE'S BURDENS

by Ingrid Auer, Spiritual Teacher

MY STORY

The raindrops on the windshield of my little red car seemed to be in competition with the tears running down my cheeks. I was on the way from my very modest flat, which I had moved into after my separation, to my estranged husband's house to pick up our two children. "OMG, how can a separation be so painful," I was sobbing. "After all, it is actually a great liberation!" Although I had so desperately longed for this separation, I was not in any way prepared for this emotional roller coaster. Let's face it, in 14 years of marriage, however good or bad it was, one does generate not only emotional, but also energetic connections with the partner.

"During every separation, invisible energetic cords connecting us with others, break," I remembered Barbara Ann Brennan's words. "The longer and the more intense a relationship is, the more pronounced become these connections, and the more painful is the heartbreak in case of a separation." This made sense to me! At that time, I was working as a successful kinesiologist. I did not only know about the physical, but also the subtle body, the aura, the meridians, and the chakras.

I had entered this marriage with a great deal of idealism and the belief in everlasting, never-ending love. I was only 22 when I married, and so was my ex-husband. Maybe I entered this marriage too naively? Maybe our lives developed too differently? Maybe we were simply too young for a marriage and two small kids?

The cars in front of me were driving slowly in a convoy along the country road. Today they did not seem to be in a hurry. "For goodness sake, get a move on!" I grumbled out loud. "At this rate, I will never get to see my children!" A mixture of anger and desperation arose in me. I have already tried so much to cope better with this separation, and still, my heart seems fit to burst. No therapy method, no flower essences, no therapy talk, and no crystals could help me be rid of this pain in my soul.

Then I thought of a friend who was constantly trying to cheer me up by suggesting that I ask the angels for help. "What? Do you mean these kitschy little angels from my childhood?" I always replied. To which my friend would always retort, "You can call them whatever you want, just talk to them!"

There I was in my car, reduced to tears and suffering, crying out loud, literally screaming, "Angels, if you are there, and can hear me, then please, please help me! Now!" Immediately my inner turmoil seemed to stop. I was stunned: "What on earth's going on?" I felt that instantly a heavenly inner peace had descended upon me. My tears dried up, and I felt lightness and joy inside me, a feeling I had not known for months. "Angels, is it you? Are you really here for me?" I exclaimed. Even though I heard no reply, the smile on my lips and in my heart was answer enough.

After my divorce and the move out of the house, I had reasonably recovered financially. Therefore I dared to take the next step by looking for a bigger flat to rent. *How, for God's sake, should I find a flat that meets my wishes?* I was thinking. *I won't easily find anything suitable in this small town of 4,000 inhabitants, where I am now living, and my children go to school.*

This was when I remembered the so-called angel letter. You write down your specific wishes and address it to the angels. I admit, this sounds a bit childish, or at the very least, reminds you of the letter children write to Santa Claus. But I was left with no other choice than to try.

I bought some particularly beautiful notepaper with specks of gold (I now realize that angels are not really interested in these sorts of things, and still fulfill wishes written on normal office paper), and sat down at the table, thinking. *What sort of flat do I actually wish for? What should it be like?* I knew I had to express my wishes very precisely so that the angels could meet my desires. Therefore, I wrote in the letter the size, the area, the number of rooms, and the rent I could afford. In the letter, I did not forget to thank the angels in advance. Then I put it in the golden envelope, sealed it, and placed it on a sideboard.

There were two supermarkets and a building supplies center in the small town where I lived. At the entrance, they had a noticeboard where people could advertise or make requests. This is where I wanted to try my luck! I wrote all the characteristics my flat should have, and which I had already expressed in my angel letter, on three medium-sized sheets of paper. Then I put some pins in my pocket and off I went.

At only the second supermarket, I was just about to pin my request on the board, when a sheet of paper caught my eye: an offer for a flat! Size, area, number of rooms, and price, perfectly corresponded with my needs and wishes. I immediately rang the number and arranged an appointment for viewing.

Walking through the flat, I knew straight away: this is it! It was perfect! Even the rent was a bit below my budget. "How many other people are interested?" I asked. The woman smiled. "We also advertised in the local paper, and since then the phone hasn't stopped ringing. All together we have 17 prospective tenants, and as you were the second to ring and the first one doesn't want it, you can have it!"

I couldn't believe my luck. My search had taken less than an hour, and now I had my dream flat. On the way back, I stopped at the flower shop, bought a beautiful bunch of flowers, and dedicated it to 'my angies' (this is what I always called my angels). Overflowing with joy and happiness, I placed it on the table, thanking the angels again, from the bottom of my heart.

Eventually, my private life was back on track again, but I was longing for a professional change. I was successfully working as a kinesiologist, booked many weeks in advance. I had 'tested' the angels effectively, and they had helped me in so many really challenging situations.

The feeling that the angels wanted something from me gradually increased. Therefore, I said to them, "Angies, tell me what I can do for you! Give me a sign, send me your impulses! I am ready, willing, and able to work for you here on earth." I could feel their presence. I felt that they had some mission for me, but what was it?

As I had started to become slightly impatient, I decided to make an angel ritual. I wanted to find out and understand what they wanted from me. Together with my best friend, I organized a few things suitable for making a ceremonial ritual: tea lights with nice holders, crystals, dried rose petals, some rose incense, a white cloth, an incense bowl, matches, paper, and pens. My friend was stuck in an unpleasant situation in her life as well, so we celebrated the ritual together, each of us for her own situation.

Before we came together for this ritual evening, we took a cleansing salt bath and put on white clothes. Then we each wrote our wish on a sheet of paper. We played meditative music, placed a big white sheet on the floor, and sprinkled rose petals on it, in the shape of a circle. We placed tea lights around the circle and lit them. We put the crystals into the center of the circle. We festively lit the charcoal in the middle of the incense bowl. We put the rose incense on top, whose sweet scent floated through the room.

An atmospheric, almost divine feeling filled the room. We invited the angels to join us and told them our hearts' desires. Then we took the sheets of paper, handing the wishes over to the angelic world by placing the paper into the incense bowl. It was a pleasant sight to see them dissolve in the flames.

What can I say? Only shortly thereafter, I was led to an angel-deep-trance-medium by 'accident' (which does not really exist). During her trance, one of my guardian angels was talking through her, "Ingrid, it is your mission to open people's hearts for us angels. And the key to this is symbols." I was flabbergasted. I had never imagined anything like that! Since then, more than 20 years have passed, and I can spread these heavenly tools all over the world. They help people during their personal and spiritual development, and also their inner healing.

Now all that was missing to make my happiness complete was my soul partner. One New Year's Eve, my friend and I made another angel ritual.

This time I wished for 'my' man in my life. Later we went out for dinner. My mood was a mixture of sadness and hope. With a glass of sparkling wine, we toasted to the year ahead. My friend, all of a sudden, said, "What's that in your hair?" It was a tiny white feather. "This is what my angels have sent me as a sign to tell me that everything will be alright." Some months later, I met the love of my life, who I am still very happy with.

THE TOOL

When was the last time you talked to angels? What, you never have? You don't believe in angels – although you would like to believe in them? Is it possible that in your childhood, you were told that angels only exist in a child's fantasy, or in church, or just at Christmas?

No matter what access to angels you have—or don't yet have—simply be open for them. There is much more between heaven and earth than what we can see, understand, measure, touch, or are able to prove scientifically. If you have not had conscious contact with angels yet, I now invite you to simply try it, to give you and them a chance.

I am often asked how we get in contact with angels and communicate with them. Some people think it involves meditating, praying, or at least remaining silent. Yes, you can do that, but it also works in everyday life, while driving your car, ironing, cooking, cutting the grass, or doing other jobs in and around the house.

Also, you do not have to know your guardian angels' names. Just call them 'my dear guardian angels.' You have at least two, maybe even four or seven, or more. The deeper you are involved with them, the more you open your heart for them, the more often you communicate with them, the more they will enter your life.

Of course, you can also invite the great archangels into your life, such as Archangel Michael, who is concerned with peace, protection, order, and justice. Or, Archangel Raphael, if someone is ill. Archangel Chamuel helps with matters of the heart or lack of self-love. Archangel Gabriel brings light into confusing situations and decisions. Archangel Uriel, if you need power, joy, and grounding, Archangel Jophiel brings more lightness and optimism, Archangel Zadkiel helps to forgive and develop spiritual awareness, or, Archangel Metatron, to discover and follow your life plan.

But let's return to getting in contact with the angels: you can talk to them like you talk to good friends, pour out your heart, cry, or write an angel letter to them (I will come back to this in a minute). However, you are allowed to be furious and vent your emotions, if you find it helps. Angels understand your feelings and are not offended by you expressing them. They have a different, higher awareness than us humans.

Once you have asked the angels something, you don't need to keep repeating it. They have a wonderful memory. Only we think that we constantly have to remind them of our wishes. But this is only human. However, it is important that you keep thanking them. This can even be an arrangement of flowers you display for them, or a beautiful crystal you dedicate to them.

And something else comes to my mind: be aware that angels are not allowed to fulfill every wish. That is because our problems and challenges in life are mainly learning steps in which our souls have chosen themselves to grow and develop. You don't like the sound of that? I admit it is a bit inconvenient. But looking back on your life, you will probably realize that it was the difficult phases in your life that moved you forward, provided that you accepted them as well as you could.

Looking back at my life today, it was exactly that time I am talking to you about now that brought me to my actual mission in life: bringing spiritual messages and tools from heaven down to earth to open people's hearts for the angels and to help them on their personal and spiritual path of development.

If you have a heart's desire, try an angel letter. By writing down what you are exactly hoping for, it focuses your thoughts. You get a clearer idea of what you want and what you don't want. Vaguely defined wishy-washy aspirations are of no use to the angels. They don't know what they should support you with. Also, your subconscious mind should focus on what you really want.

As I mentioned before, you should not forget that the angels cannot fulfill every wish. It may be that the problem you want to have solved by the angels is part of your personal learning process and a developing step. And they are not allowed to take these away from you. However, the angels will be at your side to walk through these difficult times with you. They support you whenever you need help. They send new people into your life who can help you if you are open and willing to accept their support.

You might sometimes have the feeling *Where are the angels now when I really need them? Have they given up on me? Or are they deaf or dumb?* Don't worry! There are times when they work in the background or prepare important encounters, which we call coincidences.

In the event that you have a special heart's desire, which is not easily fulfilled, or needs all possible attention and help from the angels, and if you are a romantic kind of person, then why not try an angel ritual? I have told you about my ritual, which helped to lead me to my life's mission. It is important you take enough time, that you remain undisturbed, and that you know exactly what you are wishing for. Before the ritual, gather together everything you need, such as a white cloth, feathers, crystals, candles or tea lights with holders, matches, dried flower petals or a flower arrangement, a bowl you can burn things in, a notepad and pen. Of course, you can also use incense or one of my Angel Aura Essences.

Have a bath or shower before the ritual, dress comfortably or festively (whatever you feel like), and spread out the cloth on the floor in front of you. Light the incense or spray the Angel Aura Essence above your head. Then place the bowl into the center, put candles or tea lights, crystals, the dried flower petals, the feathers, and the flower arrangement all around. Then write your heart's desire on a sheet of paper and fold it. Place it on your heart, asking the angels for support and the fulfillment of your wish. Afterward put the letter into a fireproof bowl, and light it festively. You can play heavenly music in the background and meditate. And don't forget to thank the angels!

Ingrid Auer is one of Europe's leading mediums, channeling messages and energized symbols and essences from the angels, Ascended Masters, Mary Magdalene, the Patron saints, and the Lemurian Goddesses. Since 1998 she has been writing spiritual books, which she has received as a medium.

At the center of her work, she manufactures high vibrating, energized symbols and essences, which are not only used by private individuals but also doctors, midwives, healing practitioners, energy practitioners, therapists, and teachers, with great success.

The energized symbols and essences have also proved to work well in the areas of pregnancy, childbirth, and childcare. Additionally, they are effective during care for the terminally ill and those who are grieving.

For many years, Ingrid Auer has been in close contact with the Ascended Master, Mary Magdalene. She publishes Mary Magdalene's messages, which she receives medially, and was offering spiritual journeys to Southern France, the center of the worship of Mary Magdalene in Europe.

Ingrid founded and manages her companies "Lichtpunkt & Ekonja" (Austria, publishing and worldwide distribution) and "Ingrid Auer LLC" (California, distribution in the US). She lives in Vienna, Austria, and Mallorca, Spain, and is a regular visitor to the US. Ingrid is also a Leadership Council Member of The Wellness Universe https://www.thewellnessuniverse.com/world-changers/ingridauer/

CHAPTER 16

CHOOSING RESILIENCE

USING YOUR BIOLOGY TO SHIFT FROM DISTRESS TO WELLBEING

by Jennifer Whitacre, MA, Empowerment Strategist,
and Trauma Specialist

MY STORY

Sometimes breathing isn't an option. As I type f a c into the address bar, I feel my chest tighten, a slight throb in my temples, and my chest clamps down so tightly my lungs can't expand. Social media triggers my anxiety, and that's become a problem since I started working virtually. I have several work-related groups and pages to visit and messages to check. The physical symptoms of anxiety start to emerge before Facebook fully loads.

Go straight to your business page, Jennifer, I mutter inside my head. *Do what you need to do, then move along.* I follow my own instructions, and I go straight to my business page and post. Then, I breathe a gentle sigh of relief as I share relevant posts to my two groups. *So far, so good,* I think, and I even smile at myself inside my head for staying focused this long. The self-adulation, however, is short-lived.

As I click the name of the next group from the left-hand column, my mind chatter kicks in and starts berating me. *Fucking Facebook again. You know you're addicted and need to give it up. Why don't you rip the Band-Aid off and get the withdrawal over with, you lazy bitch!*

Over the years, I took the voices of my abusers into my head, and I made them my own. Because the degradation and negativity were so much a part of my daily life, those messages didn't seem odd or unusual to me. That's just how people talked to each other. It wasn't limited to my family; this wasn't unusual behavior in the community where I grew up. Because of my upbringing, verbal abuse was normalized. I was pushing 30 when I started to realize this isn't everyone's normal. This realization coincided with my decision to move out of my hometown. A change of environment, a new circle of friends and neighbors, and a new work culture are what opened my eyes to a different, softer, and gentler approach.

That was a hard time in my life and looking back, I can understand why. I did my best to fit in with a new group of friends and colleagues, and ultimately, I didn't know how. I simply didn't have the tools I needed to manage my own emotions when stress and anxiety hijacked me. By the time I learned skills to become aware of and manage my dysfunctional patterns of thoughts and behavior, they were already a normalized part of myself. As I currently understand it, there's a good chance my inner abuser will never go away. The best I can do is notice it and work with it in the moment. Redirecting these thoughts in real-time is what creates new neural pathways, and the more I'm able to catch and redirect myself, the stronger those neural pathways will grow—like a muscle.

Now, I find myself staring at my laptop and wondering, *What was I doing? Why did I come here?* I notice agitation welling-up inside as the abuser continues, *You did it again! You said you were going to focus, and you couldn't do it, could you?* No, I couldn't, and I understand why I couldn't. I understand the physiology of trauma, and I know my nervous system just hijacked me. And yet, that intellectual understanding isn't enough to override the felt sense of the nervous system when it gets triggered. Along with that felt sense comes the story I tell myself—the one that repeats like a broken record. *You're not good enough. You're stupid. No one likes you. Only an idiot would keep doing this again and again.*

Then, the negotiator speaks up. *I want to be done with this feeling. I want to do my work without all the anxiety like everyone else does. Let's take steps to get there.* This is the solution-focused, forward-thinking aspect of my mind. Upon hearing it, I breathe a little sigh of relief. It's not just this part of me that wants this; I want this, too. I'm exhausted by the reminders of the past that live in my body. I notice my mind wanting to focus again, so I decide to keep going. I sustain that calmness and focus for two more groups I need to visit. Then, I check my notifications, and it becomes nearly impossible to distinguish between what's work-related and what's personal.

In a split-second, I can feel the sinking feeling in my gut combined with a panicky sensation in my chest that feels like I'm falling and can't catch myself. It takes my breath away as my chest clamps-down, restricting the capacity of my lungs and leaving me with only shallow breath. My heart begins to race, and I feel heat emanating from my core, creating an irritating hot flash. My normal practice of meditating, box breathing, grounding, and centering is not accessible to me; the sensation is too big, and it overtook me too fast. The shame monster reared its ugly head, my sense of safety left my body, and I'm in a full-blown stress response.

My body has shifted into autopilot, and I'm no longer in the driver's seat. It's an all-too-familiar, robotic-like state I find myself in. I click notification after notification, commenting on articles, liking memes, and reading the daily rants and confessions of my friends. Despite knowing I have work to do, I keep going, unable to override the autopilot. The next notification I click takes me back to my business page, and I start to snap out of it.

Once I catch myself, I pause long enough to reach for my cup of tea and take a drink. My cup of tea is a resource, a pleasant reminder. As I take a sip, I shift my attention to the inside. I notice the temperature of the liquid is warm, but not hot. I've been dissociated longer than I imagined. I follow the sensation as the cup touches my bottom lip, the liquid gently pours into my mouth, and I hold it there for a brief moment as I set the teacup back on its coaster. Then, I swallow and allow my attention to follow the liquid as it descends my esophagus into my stomach. I follow the sensation with each drink of tea when I notice a spontaneous breath. Something shifted, and I feel more aware and alert.

I take another moment to look around my office and notice all of the wonderful resources I have around me. To an outsider, my resources look like trinkets, rocks, and toys that clutter my space. To me, however, these resources are reminders of what brings me joy, peace, calm, and clarity. I have a feather at my desk that I found on the ground. I think it might be a mourning dove feather. Feathers are gentle reminders of my love for nature, my bird feeder station, and the variety of birds that visit, as well as the other critters, like skunks and squirrels, that eat whatever morsels fall to the ground. As I gaze at that little feather, I'm briefly transported to one of my favorite places, my back porch, where I can visualize my backyard. I subtly and intentionally shift my focus, now noticing all of the sights, sounds, smells, tastes, and sensations that I can recall. I'm able to conjure images of blue jays, nuthatches, finches, eastern bluebirds, downy woodpeckers, and cardinals. It brings a smile to my face thinking about the crows and squirrels squabbling over peanuts. It feels like I'm there, seeing the vibrant green leaves, hearing the crows cawing, noticing the bright red feathers of the cardinal, and feeling the breeze.

As my body starts to experience what my mind is seeing, I do another subtle, internal shift and notice the sensations my body is experiencing on the inside. As I stay with this visualization, I notice an expansive sensation in my chest, and a softening in my neck and shoulders as the clamp on my chest eases its grip. Wow—I didn't even notice my neck and shoulders until they started to relax. A deeper breath accompanies that expansion and relaxation, creating a greater sense of calm throughout my body. I still can't manage a full belly breath, and that's okay. The deeper breath is a step in the right direction, and I notice my gratitude for taking as deep a breath as I can in the moment. The kindness I've directed at myself helps even more, and the next breath is slightly deeper with a long, softening exhale that allows me to sink into my seat.

As I notice the chair under my butt, it comes to my awareness that I hadn't been noticing my lower body at all. The sensation of being grounded brings me to a pause as I notice the clamp wanting to tighten my chest again. I pause long enough to acknowledge the present threat of the clamp, and also to notice what else is true. In addition to the clamp, I am still noticing the expansive and relaxing sensations as well as the chair under my butt. With all of this within my awareness simultaneously, I have a choice about what to pay attention to, and I choose the expansive sensation. I focus all of my attention on the expansiveness in my chest. I notice it starts to grow as all of the other sensations start to dissipate. In my mind's eye, I picture the spotlight shining on the expansiveness while all of the other sensations that are still onstage fall into the shadows. They're not being ignored or pushed aside; they're simply not in the spotlight at the present moment.

Where I focus my attention is what grows. To me, the sensations that are expansive, relaxing, and calming are the flowers in my internal garden, while the sensations like a racing heart, shallow breathing, and a tight, clamping chest are the weeds. I get to choose what grows bigger by being mindful of what I pay attention to on the inside, and this is empowering to me. The more I notice my own empowerment, the more the expansive and calming sensations grow.

I've got this! I think to myself as I expand my awareness back into my office. I give myself a few moments to reorient to the room. Even though I didn't close my eyes, I was still transported somewhere else in my mind, and it's important I give myself a moment to land. I take in the sights, sounds, and smells around me, and the chair under my butt comes back into my awareness. I'm more grounded and embodied than I was before, without actually forcing myself to do a grounding or breathing technique to make it happen. The spontaneity of the internal shift is what makes this simple resiliency practice such a powerful one. There is no forcefulness, no leading, no agenda, and no sense of failure when it doesn't work the way it's "supposed to." There's only noticing what's present and choosing from there, so it's impossible to go wrong.

THE TOOL

CHOOSING RESILIENCE

I learned the skills of the Community Resiliency Model (CRM)® over a year ago, and they've changed my life for the better. I still get triggered, and that will never go away because I can't control what triggers me. I can control how I respond to those triggers, and the resiliency skills have proven effective because they're based in science and biology.

We humans are hard-wired to notice threat because it's part of our survival instinct, and when our autonomic functioning takes control, it continuously scans for danger. Seek, and ye shall find. I was tired of scanning for danger, and a resiliency practice is how I consciously trained myself to seek pleasant sensations that I previously wasn't aware of. Because this aspect of the self is part of our unconscious mind, it's non-verbal and doesn't respond to words. It responds to sensations, and the sensations that get the most attention create the strongest neural pathways. This is why noticing what else is true is vitally important. The loudest sensation is usually the most unpleasant one, and it can quickly overtake the mind when you pay too much attention to it, much like the weeds that strangle your garden. Pleasant emotions and sensations require nurturing, care, and attention—like slower-growing flowers, fruits, vegetables, and bushes—if they are to grow and thrive. The more you consciously divert your attention more fully on the flowering, more pleasant, and fruitful sensations, the more you nurture and fertilize their growth. You're not ignoring the weeds; you're tending to them as they arise, and nurturing the plants, or neural pathways, of your choosing.

Here are simple steps you can do now to begin laying a foundation for resiliency. Practice when you are feeling emotionally balanced to make these techniques more accessible when you are experiencing anxiety and overwhelm.

RESOURCING

A resource is anything that makes you feel calm, pleasant, peaceful, strong, or resilient. A resource can be external (a person, a place, an animal), internal (a spiritual belief, a positive characteristic, a good memory, a spiritual guide) or imagined (a superhero, a character or setting from a book or movie, or anything you can envision). Resources provide comfort, joy, peace, or happiness, and it's important to have resources available to help build resilience.

Discover resources by answering these simple questions:

- What or who gives you strength, peace, or joy in your life?
- What or who nurtures you?
- What or who uplifts you?

Use as much sensory language as you can to describe your resources. How does your resource look, sound, feel, smell, taste? Enlist as many senses as possible when describing your resource and notice what sensations and emotions you experience on the inside as you go through this exercise.

You may notice pleasant, unpleasant, or neutral sensations as you do this. Simply notice all the sensations that come up and choose to focus your attention on the sensations that you consider to be neutral or pleasant. Avoid trying to make any unpleasantness go away. Simply notice it and shift your attention to what else is true—to the neutral or more pleasant places. The more resources you build, the more you condition yourself to seek resources. Remember, seek, and ye shall find. Resourcing helps pave neural pathways that seek resources rather than threats.

HELP NOW! STRATEGIES

When closing your eyes, focused breathing, and grounding don't feel safe because the anxiety is too big, return to the basics. Help Now! strategies are accessible when there is too much stress, anxiety, and anger, or when you're feeling numb, fatigued, and dissociated from your body. These strategies can help bring more clarity and focus to your thinking mind.

Some basic Help Now! strategies include:

• Drink a glass of water, juice, or tea.

  This practice helps signal your digestive processes, which can ease the stress response. As you drink, notice what's happening on the inside. Are there any changes in what you're sensing, experiencing, or thinking? Pay attention to subtle shifts, not just big ones.

• Look around the room or space and notice anything that grabs your attention.

  Scan for colors, textures, materials, decorations, photos, pets, books, or anything that catches your eye. What about that caught your eye? Perhaps there is a fond memory of when you acquired that thing? As you consider what drew your attention, notice any shifts in the sensations you are experiencing on the inside.

• Count backward from 20.

  Count backward slowly, paying attention to any subtle shifts you experience on the inside with each number you count down.

- Touch a surface.

  Notice the texture: hard, soft, flexible, rigid, rough, squishy, smooth, sticky, etc. Pay attention to textures and surfaces that elicit neutral or more pleasant sensations.

- Walk around.

  Notice your feet making contact with the floor or ground. Which experience is more pleasant, walking quicker, slower, or at your normal pace?

With all of these techniques, it's important to notice the sensations you experience on the inside. This can be challenging at first, and it gets easier the more you practice. The more you practice, the more proficient you become. The more proficient you become, the more capacity you'll have to manage your anxiety and stress in the moment and on the go.

Please remember that this is a powerful practice that has multiple important components. I've given you a few foundational tools you'll need for this journey—tools that will help you shift from distress to wellbeing. There are more layers and levels to this practice if you're interested in mastering it. Remember to visit my resource link so that you can explore those next steps.

 Jennifer Whitacre is an Empowerment Strategist, a Trauma Specialist, a CRM® Skills Trainer, and a Body Language Trainer. A true lifelong learner, Jennifer has a stack of certifications and credentials too numerous to list. She's also a dot-connector and pattern-spotter, which makes each workshop, speaking engagement, or private session uniquely catered to the audience at hand. Her medium is subtlety, and she is gifted at helping her clients and students identify early emotional and behavioral warning signs that, when overlooked or excused away, can become a bigger issue down the road.

Jennifer was born breech, has mild dyslexia, and has been called a Heyoka by her shamans. Likewise, her brain works differently, and she's the perfect person to seek out when you're stuck in a rut and need to see from a different perspective. Naturally gifted at seeing the different shape of things, Jennifer can help you get beyond your story to discover truth.

Jennifer is honored to be the mother of a handsome, intelligent, young man; and she lives in Columbus, Ohio with her three black cats and a backyard full of birds, squirrels, deer, coyotes, and other ravine critters.

Connect with Jennifer: https://www.thewellnessuniverse.com/world-changers/jenniferwhitacre/

CHAPTER 17

MOVING MEDITATION

MIND-BODY BALANCE THROUGH INTUITIVE MOVEMENT

by Jill Alman-Bernstein, MFA, Intuitive Empowerment Coach

MY STORY

Breath and movement have always stirred my mind, body, and soul. The dancer in my heart has propelled me through life, grand jete after grand jete, pirouette after pirouette, toes pointed, arms outstretched like wings: the air lifting my spirit, rhythm pulsing in my soul.

I found yoga and yogic breathing along the way, and though I got a lot from that practice, something was missing. I was definitely a Vinyasa girl, loving the flow of movement, but I missed the "dance." My body ached for a movement practice that was creative, fluid, meditative, and intuitive.

I was introduced to the "Chakras." Intrigued, I researched and learned as much as possible, looking at how I could connect them to my own personal breath and movement practice.

I tuned in to cycles, signs, and synchronicities. The number 28 was significant; it resonated. I was born on the 28th. There are 28 days in the lunar cycle and 28 days in the divine feminine cycle. I thought: 28 deep long sustained breaths. There are seven primary chakras; I played with four breaths for each. I explored how it felt to consciously breathe 28 times in a row, to each day take 28 breaths before I did anything else, and allow movement to organically come from each breath.

When we connect to our intuitive self through our breath, we are able to calm the nervous system through conscious awareness and alleviate tension and stress in the body. In that process, we find clarity for our unique and authentic self-expression. We connect the breath, voice, and body to the heart, mind, and spirit to heal and empower us.

That is the premise of this Tool. This Moving Meditation uses conscious breath to create the impulse for the body and intuitively inform and guide movement that is authentic, creative, calming, and healing. The number of breaths has been expanded from the original 28 breaths to allow for a more embodied and integrated fully expressed experience.

"Behind the visible movement, there is another movement,
one which cannot be seen, which is very strong,
on which the outer movement depends.
If this inner movement were not so strong,
the outer one would not have any action."

–Jeanne de Salzmann

"Breath is the link between mind and body.
Conscious breathing heightens awareness and deepens relaxation."

– Dan Brule

THE TOOL

Find a relaxed stance, with your feet comfortably apart, weight evenly on both feet, soft knees.

Begin taking gentle breaths. Inhale through your nose, exhale through your mouth. Inhale through your nose, exhale through your mouth. Find the rhythm of your breath.

Connect your feet to the floor, to the earth. Wake up the soles of your feet so that you really feel the floor; roll back and forth from your toes, through the balls of your feet, through your arches, to your heels, and back through to your toes.

Allow your knees to be loose. Give a few gentle bounces and really plant your feet into the ground. Imagine that you are dropping an anchor from the soles of your feet down into the earth's core. Visualize a cord. Give it a color that has meaning for you, that brings you warmth, confidence. The cord connects you to the vital source energy that is in the earth below you.

Inhale, and now as you allow your knees to gently bend, exhale, blow out your breath, hear your exhale.

Then as you inhale, begin to gently straighten your knees, imagine bringing the energy up from the earth, into your feet, into your ankles, into your calves, through your knees, into your thighs, and into your sacrum — the base of your spine, your Root Chakra. Exhale.

Think:

- Grounding
- Safety
- Stability
- Self-Confidence

Allow the energy to fill that space, warm that area, as you take four breaths:

Inhale, and straighten the knees, **locate** the Root Chakra, exhale and allow the knees to gently bend.

Inhale, straighten the knees, pulling the energy up through your feet and legs into the Root Chakra, **sense** the energy that is blocked and needs to be cleared, exhale, gently bend the knees, and send the energy back down, feeling the weight of the anchor, the rush of the energy through the cord.

Inhale, and **awaken** the Root Chakra as you pull the energy up straightening your knees, exhale, release the breath and the knees.

Last breath, inhale and gently straighten, **deepen** the breath and the energy that you bring in, and exhale, release the breath and the knees.

Continue with gentle breaths as you allow the energy to integrate.

Allow your hips to begin a gentle sway. Let your arms flow freely.

Visualize the anchor, the cord, now coming up through your Root Chakra into the area of your hips and pelvis, right below the navel, into your Sacral Chakra.

Allow the sway of your hips and arms, your body's movement, to explore this area.

Find your:

- Creativity
- Sensitivity
- Sexuality
- Emotional Well-Being
- Self Expression

Inhale and let your hips and arms sway, **locate** the Sacral Chakra, exhale.

Inhale, let your hips and arms sway, **sense** the energy in the chakra, exhale.

Inhale, sway your body, **awaken** the chakra, exhale.

Inhale, and sway, **deepen** your awareness of the Sacral Chakra, exhale.

Pull the energy up to your waist area and move the sway to a gentle twist, allowing the arms to join the movement your body's way, swaying and twisting as your body feels it wants to move. Come back to center. Put one hand on your upper belly where your diaphragm sits. Connect to your breath and the Solar Plexus Chakra.

This is your:

- Personal Power
- Identity
- Wisdom
- Self-Esteem

Inhale and twist to the left, **locate** the Solar Plexus Chakra, exhale and twist to the right, and float back to center.

Inhale and twist to the right, **sense** the energy of your breath, exhale and twist to the left, and float back to center.

Inhale and twist to the left, **awaken** the Solar Plexus, exhale and twist to the right, and float back to center.

And inhale and twist to the right, and **deepen** your awareness of the energy in this chakra, and exhale and twist to the left and float back to center.

Move the energy up. Open your chest, breathing deep conscious breaths into your heart.

Inhale and open your arms at shoulder height, extending them out to your sides, and thrust your chest, your Heart Chakra forward.

Locate your Heart Chakra.

Here is your:

- Balance
- Love
- Self-love
- Healing

Exhale and bring your arms back, crossing your right arm over the left, hands grasping the opposite shoulder in a hug like position.

Inhale and open your arms at shoulder height, extending them out to your sides, and thrust your chest, your Heart Chakra forward.

Sense the energy in your heart.

Exhale and bring your arms back, crossing your left arm over the right, hands grasping the opposite shoulder in a hug like position.

Inhale, and open your arms at shoulder height, extending them out to your sides, thrusting your chest, your Heart Chakra forward.

Awaken your heart.

Exhale and bring your arms back, crossing your right arm over the left, in a hug like position.

And last inhale, open your arms at shoulder height, extending them out to your sides, and thrust your chest, your Heart Chakra forward.

Deepen the awareness and connection to your heart energy.

And as you exhale, bring your arms back, crossing your left arm over the right, hugging yourself one more time.

Take a few breaths to integrate.

Allow a gentle sway to begin from your feet, still connected, anchored to the earth energy, the sway moves up through your ankles, calves, knees, thighs, to your Root Chakra, and to your Sacral Chakra. Breathe and feel into your sway.

What does your body need? Connect to your breath, to your body's vital source energy. Allow your movement to find the connection intuitively, naturally, authentically. Allow that energy to move into your Solar Plexus, your chest, your heart.

Come to a centered and balanced stance. Let your arms hang loosely at your side. Take a few gentle, conscious, connected breaths.

Now move the energy up to your throat.

To open the Throat Chakra you must not only breathe with movement but vocalize.

Allow your jaw to drop open so that your lips are slightly parted.

Practice taking a few breaths here. Inhale through the nose, and as you exhale through your mouth, allow your breath to produce a sound, any sound, whatever sound your body and breath wish to make.

Now you'll add the movement.

As you inhale, raise your chin and head up so that you are gazing at the ceiling or sky, and as you exhale, allow your breath to sigh or make a sound, your head and chin fall, your chin tucks into your throat.

Ask for:

- Knowledge
- Inner truth
- Communication
- Personal power

You'll take four conscious breaths:

Inhale and raise your chin and head, **locate** the Throat Chakra as you open and expose the throat, and exhale, release a sigh or sound as you drop the head, tuck the chin, and release the breath.

Second breath. Inhale and raise your chin and head, as you open and expose the throat, **sense** the energy that needs to be brought in or cleared, and exhale, release a sigh or sound as you drop the head, tuck the chin, and release the breath.

Inhale and raise your chin and head, as you open and expose the throat, **awaken** your voice, and exhale, release the head, tuck your chin, release the breath, and a sound.

And the last breath, **deepen** the breath and awareness.

Inhale and raise your chin and head, opening and exposing the throat, and exhale, release the head, tuck the chin, release the breath, and a sound.

Bring your head back to center and take two more breaths to integrate.

As you inhale, think about bringing that cord of color, that energy from the earth, all the way up through your body, into your throat.

Inhale, and exhale, and just release your breath and whatever intuitive sound you are finding.

And again, inhale, and exhale, releasing your breath and your sound.

Let your arms float up from your hips, and extend out to your side and then up over your head.

Bring your palms together and then bring your palms down, pressing your thumbs to the center of your forehead, to your Third Eye Chakra.

Allow:

• Intuition

• Mysticism

• Imagination

• Understanding

Inhale, into your thumbs and **locate** your Third Eye. Exhale, let your palms and arms float down and open and extend out, then circle up, bringing palms together and palms and thumbs back to your Third Eye.

Second breath. Inhale and **sense** the power in your Third Eye. Palms together, thumbs pressed to the center of your forehead. Exhale. Release your hands and arms down, out to your sides, and circle back up over your head, bringing your palms together, and your thumbs to your Third Eye.

And inhale. **Awaken** your higher self. Palms together, thumbs pressed to the center of your forehead. And exhale, release your hands and arms down, out to your sides, and circle back up over your head, bringing your palms together, thumbs to your Third Eye.

Last breath. Inhale, palms together, and thumbs pressed to the center of your forehead, **deepen** your connection to your Third Eye. And exhale, release your hands and arms down, out to your sides, and circle back up over your head, bringing your palms together, thumbs to rest at your Third Eye.

Take a moment to let your body and breath come together, integrating the energy, the awareness.

Breathe into your Third Eye. Allow your palms, hands, and arms to freely find their path of movement. Do they want to reach up to the sky or float out in a wave or down bringing the energy of the breath through your fingertips? Do your hips want to sway or circle? Do your shoulders want to gently be pulled up and down or roll together or one at a time? Let your ankles, calves, and knees bend and rock gently, testing your body-breath connection. Allow your torso to fill with your breath and twist and unwind as you exhale. Let these breaths and movements be fluid, inhaling and exhaling the breath, the movement, adding voice to amplify the vibration and resonance.

In your own time, begin to bring the movements smaller, elongate your breath, extending the inhale, lengthening the exhale. Take a few very slow breaths and come to your centered and balanced stance. Find your anchor and that cord that connects you like an umbilical cord to the earth and source energy. Continue your slow, conscious breaths. Visualize the cord and its color, seeing it come up through each of the chakras and areas of your body that you have focused on, through the legs to the base of the spine, your Root, to your Sacral Chakra, to your Solar Plexus, to your heart, to your throat, to your Third Eye.

Stand relaxed and tall.

You are at your Crown Chakra now. This is where all the information from all the chakras merge.

It is here that you connect with your higher consciousness, the oneness of you, and of the universe. Energy flows freely through you. Embrace divine inspiration and divine creativity. There is a deep sense of peace, serenity. Be inspired! See the beauty, unity, find awareness and enlightenment.

Place one palm over the other on the top of your head and inhale.

Exhale and reach your arms up to the sky, gaze and face to the sky, stretch your fingertips.

Inhale and bring your palms back one over the other to the top of your head.

Exhale and allow your chin, head, and arms to drop, head folding into your chest, the weight of your head carrying it down, body bending at the waist, knees bending, arms and head dropping down to wherever they land.

Take an inhale and exhale in this position.

Inhale and begin rolling up slowly, vertebrae by vertebrae, to a relaxed standing position and exhale.

And again.

One palm over the other on the top of your head and inhale.

Exhale and reach and look to the sky.

Inhale and bring your palms back one over the other to the top of your head.

Exhale and allow your chin, head, and arms to drop, head folding into your chest, the weight of your head carrying it down, body bending at the waist, knees bending, arms and head dropping down to wherever they land.

Take an inhale and exhale.

Inhale and begin rolling up slowly, vertebrae by vertebrae, to a relaxed standing position and exhale.

Place one palm over the other on the top of your head and inhale.

Exhale and reach your arms up to the sky, gaze and face to the sky, stretch your fingertips.

Inhale and bring your palms back one over the other to the top of your head.

Exhale and allow your chin, head, and arms to drop, head folding into your chest, the weight of your head carrying it down, body bending at the waist, knees bending, arms and head dropping down to wherever they land.

Take an inhale and exhale in this position.

Inhale and begin rolling up slowly, vertebrae by vertebrae, to a relaxed standing position and exhale.

And, last time.

Place one palm over the other on the top of your head and inhale.

Exhale and reach your arms up to the sky.

Inhale and bring your palms back one over the other to the top of your head.

Exhale and allow your chin, head, and arms to drop, head folding into your chest, the weight of your head carrying it down, body bending at the waist, knees bending, arms and head dropping down to wherever they land.

Take an inhale and exhale.

Inhale and begin rolling up slowly, vertebrae by vertebrae, to a relaxed standing position and exhale.

Close your eyes and just breathe, feeling into every part of your body, noticing each place where you focused attention, breath, and movement.

Now inhale. Circle your arms out and up over your head, bring your palms together, and then down to your chest, exhale, thumbs to heart.

You'll do this three more times, each time a little more slowly.

Inhale. Circle your arms out and up over your head, bring your palms together, and then down to your chest, exhale, thumbs to heart.

Inhale. Circle your arms out and up over your head, bring your palms together, and then down to your chest, exhale, thumbs to heart.

And last time, very slowly.

Inhale. Circle your arms out and up over your head, bring your palms together, and then down to your chest, exhale, thumbs to heart.

Open your eyes, take a big inhale, and exhale, blowing out your breath with a sound, and step into your day!

Jill Alman-Bernstein has been a student and teacher of movement and dance for five decades. She studied classical ballet, lyrical, modern, and jazz dance, and Iyengar and Vinyasa yoga. Ms. Alman-Bernstein is trained in the voice, breath, and movement techniques of Arthur Lessac, Kristin Linklater, and Alexander, and is a Nia White Belt. Her somatic work focuses on connecting to the authentic self through conscious breath, voice, and movement.

When she is not moving her body, Ms. Alman-Bernstein is working with clients at the intersection of intuition, empowerment, and transformation. As an Intuitive Empowerment Coach and Soul Realignment Certified Practitioner, she is a passionate and intuitive guide, assisting you to align with your highest path and purpose. She is an inspirational writer and deep sea soul diver, and the creator of the social media platform I Must Be A Mermaid, focusing on inspiration, personal growth, and spiritual development.

Ms. Alman-Bernstein loves walking on the beach, nature, theatre, romantic comedies, laughing with her best friends, and of course dancing! She lives on Martha's Vineyard with her family, and strives to breathe in the beauty of each and every day.

https://www.thewellnessuniverse.com/world-changers/jill-alman-bernstein/

CHAPTER 18

THE 7-SECOND MINDSHIFT™

RETRAIN YOUR BRAIN FOR CALM ON-DEMAND

by Donna Blevins, PhD

MY STORY

This is the first time I'm publicly coming out of the closet. I have a secret to share with you. Well, two secrets. I am a convicted felon, and poker saved my life.

The crossroads of poker and transformation surfaced in 1996. Without discovering the game, today I would be dead from stress. Or worse yet, suicide.

When life deals crappy cards, it sucks, but you always have choices. Play full out and take calculated risks; bemoan your fate and hold on even when you know you have a losing hand; or fold early and fold often.

While competing in a poker tournament, when I make a stupid call and become "tilted"—that place of emotional imbalance—there is no way I can say, "Please excuse me. Give me half an hour while I recompose, meditate, and calm down."

Traditional meditation never worked for me at the poker table. There is no time. The game happens fast, and there is a need for speed. Time is a commodity that is in short supply while in the game.

Whether or not you've ever played a hand of poker, imagine for a moment you're in a tournament. You've just made an ultra-stupid mistake—an epic blunder.

You're sitting there with cards in your hands, beating yourself up about that idiot move. Effectively, you are anchoring your mistake and convincing yourself that you are a failure and unworthy.

Do you ever find yourself uttering self-defeating words such as: "What an idiot I am!" "Why do I keep doing such stupid stuff?" "When will I ever stop being a fool?"

What if you realized that the hand you are holding is the only reality that exists? Your only choice in life is how you play the cards you are dealt.

The past is gone. Those cards were folded. Future cards are not yet here. You realize the future never comes. There is only NOW.

This realization came to me in the middle of a hand. In an instant, through the simple process of shifting my awareness into the moment, I discovered the calm and peace of mindfulness, which saved my life.

As I took a long, deep breath, my hyperactive self-loathing inner voice became still. Quiet. Calm wrapped her arms around me, and I was at peace.

Could calm be as simple as one single breath?

ASK AND YE SHALL RECEIVE

Poker was a diversion from my never-ending seventeen-hour days as the real estate management broker for the US Department of Veteran Affairs in five counties in Florida. I loved my life and hated what I did.

Can you imagine the feeling of overwhelm that comes with taking custody of nearly two hundred properties in a single day?

I loved helping people get their first-ever home and despised that it came at the cost of other people losing their homes. I hated being the one evicting families living in properties the VA had acquired because of the foreclosure process.

By the time I became the guardian of the properties, all the paperwork and court filings were complete. However, two in ten homes were still occupied. One eviction was the decisive point that changed my life.

Thinking back, I remember that soul-wrenching day as if it were yesterday. As I write this, my heart still aches.

Storms rumbled loudly in the distance. As I drove to the neighborhood, I felt the gloomy clouds following me. With each turn, it seemed they turned in unison—what a dreadful way to start a summer's day on this beautiful Gulf Coast of Florida.

The eviction was scheduled around 9 am, and the day before, I reminded the crew, "Let's be sure to get it done after the neighbors are gone to work, but before kids on the block get home from school."

My heart raced, and breathing quickened as I turned the corner and saw the homeowner back out of the garage. I stopped the car half a block away and watched the garage door lower, and wondered, "Am I at the wrong address?"

There was a bicycle lying by the driveway. The yard had just been mowed.

A few minutes after she drove away, the deputy sheriff arrived, and I asked him, "Has all the paperwork been served? Is this the right house?"

He nodded yes and said, "Right place. It's on the front door. All the servings are posted there. It started over nine months ago. It's taken longer than required, and today, we must take action."

Walking up to the front door, I felt sick. The curtains were open, and the inside looked like the family-next-door everybody wants.

As a government agent trained as a locksmith, picking locks was usually a snap. This time, my hands shook. The deputy stood over me as I struggled with the front door lock. Finally, the deputy said, "Just drill it. I have to go."

Darkness saturated my soul as I drilled and thought, *I can't do this anymore.*

Inside I discovered nothing was packed. Absolutely nothing. All the closets were full of clothes, and everything was tidy inside. Based on the clothes and possessions in the bedrooms, it looked like two kids, maybe 10 and 12, and Mom.

How could she ignore the notices? I kept wondering.

Everything had to be moved to the curb. Furniture. Clothes. Toys. Food. Everything. I fell into the black hole of self-blame as I directed a six-man crew to be careful with everything but hurry it up.

That was part of my job. That was what the VA told me to do. That day turned a pure love-hate relationship into not-no-more. I was in despair.

Standing there at that curb looking at the evicted-family's household of belongings, the rain came pounding down. Thunder rolled. Lightning flashed.

Pulling money out of my pocket, I sent the crew to get tarps. Tears ran down my face, and I shouted into the storm, *"How do I get out of this? I. Want. Out. NOW!"*

When you ask and declare, you WILL receive.

In a ridiculously short time after I made the request, two US Marshals appeared at my real estate office with a subpoena in hand, and said, "Donna Blevins, you have been served."

I was dismayed to learn that an agent had made a mistake on a contract. As the broker of record, I was charged with a felony. The buck stopped with me.

Overwhelmed with red tape and the workload of taking custody of and managing properties, I was blinded by the chaos. The paperwork as a government real estate management broker was grueling. I had failed to catch the mistake. A single error was the reason for the charges, and with seemingly no other choice, I accepted the blame.

Rather than spending tens of thousands on lawyers, dragging my family into the mire, and crushing my own spirit, I plead to a white-collar felony, closed the office, paid a fine, and was on probation for a year.

Sounds simple, right?

I had no idea that that decision of pleading to a felony had the power to taint my life and cloud my self-worth, undermine my self-esteem, and demolish my self-confidence for the rest of my life. Guilt, judgment, blame, and shame prevailed.

At the moment I am writing this chapter, here and now, I take back my power. As I write, I am canceling the emotional effect of being a convicted felon.

Shame evaporates as I declare, "I love who I am. I love who I have become. I am me because of what I have experienced and the lessons that I have learned. I am of service to others."

POKER BACK STORY

First, let me be clear. Poker is a great metaphor for life, and I find comfort in the similarities.

In both poker and life, we continually make a series of choices, one decision after another. We strive to minimize our errors armed only with incomplete information and to achieve desired results.

As I learned poker, I experienced moments of joy and reemergence of confidence during the extended negotiation of the felony plea and yearlong probation. It's like, "Okay. I pled guilty. Now let's get on with it! For God's sake, just deal another hand!"

Looking back, I still shake my head in wonderment. My life was transforming. Evolving. One life was ending as another one began. I had no idea at the time the significance of the overlap.

After five years trying to survive during stress-filled days as the management broker, I stumbled onto poker—a simple card game played by people. In the process, I realized that poker is actually a people game played with cards, a welcomed distraction during one of the pivotal times in my life.

In my late 40s and the first time I picked up cards, I had no idea how to play or what constituted a winning hand. After complaining to my husband that there was little to read for beginning poker players, he said, "Maybe you writing about learning the game as a new player would be good for you and the reader. You're the fastest learner I've ever known! Just write about it."

As a result, I became a poker journalist and have been since 1998, the year I plead to the felony. For me, poker became my framework to grow as a human being. To reclaim my self-worth.

As I mastered the game, my world improved. I was stronger, more confident, even happier. Other people noticed and wanted to know how that happened. They wanted some of whatever it was I was on, and, just like that, I became a poker coach focusing on improving people's lives.

Over the last two decades, with the advent of the internet, a priceless collection of poker coaches has emerged. Most of them focus on strategy and left-brain math-based statistical analysis. As the first poker mindset coach, I introduced the concept of the mind game in the early 2000s, and mental coaches evolved.

To clarify, I'm both a left-brain and a right-brain coach. I balance pragmatics with my intuitive sense. Regardless of the industry, I use the concept of game-theory during private sessions and on the one-to-many platforms.

Coming from a religious background with strong work ethics, I "smuggle spirituality" to the poker table and into sessions with all types of clients. When I say that people chuckle and ask, "What does that mean?"

Others call the process life-balance. For me, it involves strengthening the mind-body-spirit connection without bringing in all the woo-woo stuff.

When we focus on just our physicality, regardless of what we are "playing"—whether in sales, speaking, coaching, or cards—we rarely fire on all cylinders. We choke. Our mental gears lock up, and we stall.

Think about learning through the whole-you. Make it a habit of exercising your mental muscles, taking care of your body first, and opening conversations with your inner wisdom.

Rather than looking at "your game" as separate and distinct from the rest of you, see it as an extension of you. From the poker table to the boardroom, one of the biggest challenges I've discovered over the years is that people try to be like someone else. They try to mimic others, rather than finding what I call "your authentic game."

"Playing your game" has nothing to do with the cards. It comes from a clear, uncluttered view of your true self.

Am I suggesting you take up the game of poker? That depends.

For poker to be therapeutic, you must play with intention and mindfulness, rather than reacting. Hmm...now that sounds like life's best game plan because it is.

The whole basis of stress is rooted in reacting to life's challenges without pausing and coming to the moment where you consider your options before consciously acting.

My intention over the years has become, "I intend to make correct decisions and remain unattached to the outcome." As poker metaphors come into the mix, my intention has evolved to include a blessing, "May the cards break in my direction and may the odds be on my side."

Face it. You never have it all. You never have all the information. Every decision we make in life is based on the limited information we have at that point in time.

YOUR BIOLOGICAL SUPERCOMPUTER

Here's the fact. Your brain is a magnificent biological supercomputer that was naturally programmed to protect you. To react quickly. To make snap decisions. Immediate reaction is our natural, automatic normal.

The problem when we continue to be in that reactive state is that our brain does not know when a perceived threat is not a saber tooth tiger. We become stressed, and our body secretes cortisol, the hormone that triggers the protective insulation of fat around our vital organs.

Thankfully, we can reprogram the underlying software within our subconscious mind as opposed to remaining reactive throughout our life.

When a negative thought comes to mind, we have less than a second before it anchors and takes root. If that sounds fast, Google the "speed of thought." You'll find that a given thought can be generated and acted on in little as one-twentieth of a second.

Crap! That IS fast.

What we think we create. Our body is the vehicle. Our mind is the operator, the driver.

Thoughts are fast. We "think them." We react to them. Thoughts bounce around in our head like ping pong balls.

We live in the middle of chaos and spend our life being reactive. We react in a split second and create more of the same.

This morning I awoke realizing that unrecognized thoughts are like a runaway freight train without an engineer, the train's driver.

Inside our brain, thoughts create new highways. The brain can learn.

With repetition, I discovered that we could literally rewire our own neural pathways. You can retrain your brain to pause and then shift to being aware before acting. You strengthen your mental muscles by developing Emotional Agility™.

In today's age, where technology has sucked us into our smartphone and down the computer's rabbit hole, we are creating stressors that damage our bodies and our mind.

Over our life, we developed the habit of being unaware and became a slave to our emotions. We trained our brain to be even more reactive. To remain unconsciously incompetent. We don't know what we don't realize we don't know.

We can retrain our brain to access calm on-demand—our place of blissful peace—by making the recognition process a habit. The habit of noticing a negative thought as it comes to mind gives you the power to shift your mindset before negativity anchors and takes root.

In short, the following process is a MindShifting™ method and is evidence-based technology. You can use it now, at this very moment. It only takes practice, just like exercising any muscle.

Let's begin.

THE TOOL

It's time to shift away from being unaware and unprepared in your quest to becoming unconsciously competent one-minute-at-a-time. Today, this lightning-fast method works for entrepreneurs, executives, healthcare teams, worker-bees, and for you—whatever you choose to do and whomever you choose to be.

Overview of the 7-Second MindShift™, also known as the Seven-Eleven Shift:

- Inhale to the count of 7
- Exhale slowly through softly pursed lips to the count of 11
- Do the 7/11 process three times
- Total time required, one minute
- Use belly breathing technique
- Expected result is increasing relaxation and lowering stress

Exhaling through pursed lips is healthy because our lungs have millions of tiny sacs that behave like little balloons. When they deflate and stick together, they require extra pressure to re-inflate, just like a balloon you once used and put away in a drawer.

If you feel you're unable to exhale to the count of 11, using the belly breathing technique is helpful. I've discovered that many people limit their oxygen intake and carbon dioxide outflow by only chest breathing, and belly breathing is a simple solution.

Belly breathing, like many other things that are new to us, may require some practice. Belly breathing is healthy, simple to learn, and relaxing.

To belly breathe, sit or lie flat in a comfortable position. Put one hand on your chest and the other on your belly just below your ribs.

As you breathe in, to the count of 7, let your belly push your hand out. Let your chest remain still and not move.

Breathe out slowly through softly pursed lips to the count of 11. Notice the hand on your belly go in, and use that muscle to push all the air out. Allow your chest to remain still.

Adding the 7-in and 11-out process helps cleanse the body.

The purpose of The 7-Second MindShift™ is:

By counting the breaths in rhythm, three breaths fit nicely within one minute.

While you are counting and noticing your breathing, you are unable to fret or worry. The more mental muscles and physical processes you bring into the method, the more you occupy your brain.

Counting for 7 seconds begins to train the brain to recognize how long 7 seconds is.

PROGRESS CONFIRMATION

Now that you have experienced this MindShift Exercise™, it's time to say the following aloud:

"Now that I have learned how to expand the anchor-time when a negative thought comes to mind from one-twentieth of a second to 7 seconds, I am becoming emotionally and mentally agile."

Using this tool, you can create a 7-Second Window of Opportunity, where you have ample time to decide what you choose to think.

Zig Ziglar said, "Donna Blevins is someone we can all look up to, both professionally and physically."

Donna Blevins is a 6-foot 5-inch tall powerhouse married to a 5-foot 3-inch Vietnam combat veteran, a man she looks up to.

As an International professional poker player, Donna candidly shares her intimate story of turning losses into wins by accessing the wisdom within those mistakes.

MindShift coach and world-class speaker, Blevins uses her earthy down-home Appalachian humor and highly original voice to teach people Emotional Agility™, a term she coined and an evidence-based technology she created that has been life-changing for many, life-saving for some.

Topping the list of her awards, she earned The Recognition Award from the Department of Veterans Affairs.

Donna got the proof that her methods work in real time on-demand when her speech was muted by a massive stroke. Her healthcare team said it would take 8-9 months before she could speak. Using her methods, she was able to speak in three short days!

She now shares her techniques worldwide by way of virtual master classes and inside her community of influencers, who are ready to learn how to MindShift On-Demand™, the proven way to retrain the brain.

https://www.thewellnessuniverse.com/world-changers/donnablevinsphd/

CHAPTER 19

KNOWING YOUR TRUE VALUE

COEXISTING IN PEACE & HARMONY WITH EGO

by Debbra Lupien, Voice of the Akashic Records

MY STORY

Nearly 70% of individuals will experience signs and symptoms of Impostor Syndrome at least once in their life.

The voice of Impostor Syndrome creeps into your psyche, taunting with words like: *You're just a pretender. You don't belong.*

That. Is. A. Lie!

As a survivor of Impostor Syndrome, I'm here to tell you that it's real and will suck all the joy out of your life if you let it. My battle with the Impostor demon was painful, devastating, and expensive.

It was also instructive and, as it turns out, an important part of my life journey.

UNIVERSAL TRUTH

Today I **know** this truth and I hope after I share my story you'll know it, trust it, and believe it; because it **is** universal **TRUTH**:

"You are an incredible being, unique in all the world. There's not another like you. Just as snowflakes are unique, so too are you.
A great deal of love, care, and intention was woven into your soul matrix.

You have the ability to bring amazing insights and world-changing knowledge to whatever endeavor you choose to be a part of.
You are a magnificent soul, and you are perfect just as you are.

Your underlying purpose is to seek out higher consciousness, find what feeds your Soul, then do it.
That is the path to bliss. That is soul nirvana.

THE SEEDS OF IMPOSTOR SYNDROME

I've always been driven. Learn more. Do more. Be more. You might say I'm a professional student.

That incessant drive meant there wasn't a whole lot of slowing down to appreciate my accomplishments or even life for that matter. It was always "onward to the next goal."

I didn't question; it was my normal. Everyone felt that — didn't they? Didn't they? If I only knew then what I know now.

In retrospect, I can see there was a black hole of neediness sucking up my joy, demanding more, more, MORE! Nothing was ever enough. **I** was never enough…until I was. At the root of Impostor Syndrome is low self-esteem.

SITTING ON TOP OF THE WORLD
(HOW I ARRIVED AT THE DOORSTEP OF IMPOSTOR SYNDROME)

In 1987, I started my first business, which was word processing. It felt great to be in control of my destiny. That was before the Internet was invented, so there was no Googling for entrepreneurial advice. It was flying by the seat of your pants; figure it out as you go.

Since I needed a way to manage my growing business efficiently, I began dabbling in database software. It wasn't long until I had a snappy custom system that functioned with push-button ease. My kind of software: does its job and gets out of the way so you can do the work that brings in revenue.

Jazzed about my creation, I began telling clients how much time it was saving me. Plus, it worked the way I wanted it to. It was unnecessary to follow someone else's rules about how to track my data. Of course, they wanted their own system, too. Once more, my business evolved, I became a custom database developer.

I remember one lady, a music rep, who had been doing all of her record-keeping the old fashioned way — on paper. When we met, she was beside herself, practically wailing: "I haven't paid my artists their royalties for more than a year!"

She pulled out handfuls of paper records from a file drawer and declared, "I desperately need to get this resolved. Can you please help me?"

The system I designed for her reduced the task to pushing a button, entering a date range, and hitting enter. Her printer fired up, and voilà, she now had a complete report compiling all those royalty payments. Her eyes grew big with astonishment as she beamed from ear to ear. An enormous undertaking now became a simple routine.

Yeah, baby! What a sweet moment! My old nemesis — low self-esteem — seemed to have been banished. I was now free to enjoy the satisfaction and success of my growing business.

Those were exciting and heady days. I was on the leading edge of database publishing and thrilled to work with some of the biggest publishers in New York City, including Little Golden Books, a treasured childhood friend. One of those pinch-me-to-make-sure-it's-real moments. I was flying high.

Around that time, a huge database software company invited selected companies to "partner" with them. They needed trusted programmers to refer their clients to. My work with database publishing had already been recognized and highlighted in their corporate marketing materials, which encouraged me to apply. Much to my astonishment, I was accepted!

That was a giant leap into the big leagues. Amazing and terrifying at the same time. It triggered my low self-esteem, which I thought had been banished. Turns out, it was simmering below the surface, just waiting for the opportunity to reappear. Worse yet. It was poised to introduce me to its evil spawn: Impostor Syndrome.

PARTNERSHIP'S A BITCH

Several times a year, we partners met with corporate to hear about the latest and greatest innovations. There was a lot of focus on best practices and sharing of programming code.

Up until then, I had been proud of my code. It was logical, simple, and effective. Pretty impressive for someone who was mostly self-taught (I felt). As I sat in those meetings observing others' code, doubt crept in. Maybe there was a reason to write code that appeared to be convoluted? Maybe mine wasn't so good after all? Maybe, maybe, maybe.

Around that same time, my business had inched up to six figures, which caused mixed feelings. Hitting that milestone really messed with my head because it was contrary to my self-identity. I had never dreamed that was even possible for me.

You see, I "only" have a degree in Secretarial Science. In fact, I was a secretary from the tiny town of Edon, Ohio. My father was a factory worker/farmer and labored for pennies. We were poor.

I had no formal training as a programmer. None of that mattered on my way to success. But now that I was comparing myself to others, my lack of credentials mattered way too much, and the proverbial rug was about to be pulled out from under me.

Each partner meeting worsened the feeling that I was a pretender to the party. What was I doing there amongst those highly educated people who were "real" programmers? When I compared my code to theirs, I judged that mine was lacking. A voice in the back of my mind screamed, amateur!

Once that taunting voice took off like a runaway freight train, there was no escaping self-condemnation. My confidence and joy were crushed. I felt as small as Alice after she took the blue pill in Wonderland. I didn't measure up. What was I even doing there?

Tormenting myself incessantly with these thoughts, I was powerless to stop.

My confidence was so shattered that I found myself at the annual developer's conference telling people I didn't belong. Unconsciously, I was probably hoping to find someone to tell me otherwise, but that didn't happen. Instead, their lack of support served to reinforce my doubts further. My developer colleagues must have thought I was having a breakdown, and I suppose in a way I was.

Or, more likely, they were giving little thought to me at all. They were absorbed with their own issues. Over the years, I've learned this is usually the case.

PICKING UP THE PIECES

Back then, I'd never heard of Imposter Syndrome, but it doesn't care if you know its name. Impostor Syndrome will eat you up and swallow you whole when you let it.

My ugly consequence of Impostor Syndrome was self-sabotaging myself right out of a successful business that I had built through grit and sheer determination. I didn't re-certify as a "partner" and stopped taking new clients. My business dissolved with barely a whimper.

Thankfully, not everyone allows Imposter Syndrome to defeat them as thoroughly as I did. Still, it's a reality to a lesser degree for nearly 70% of us, which brings us back around to the Universal truth I mentioned earlier: You are a magnificent being, unique in all the world. Don't let anyone tell you otherwise — **especially you**!

When you understand the truth of who you are, it becomes illogical to compare yourself to anyone. There is no one like you. If you must compare, then compare with yourself. Are you growing and expanding? If yes, terrific, keep doing that. If not, why not, and what are you going to do about it?

That nugget of truth is the key to more peace, happiness, and success. It's the key to being more fully who you intended to be in this lifetime.

REINVENTING MYSELF

Over the next ten years, I tried various businesses with little success. Recovering from that level of devastation is no trivial matter. However, in time I bounced back better than ever. Way better as it turns out!

The turning point was when I discovered the Akashic Records. In that moment, it felt as if the heavens opened up, and the angels sang an aria of: "Welcome home."

Shortly thereafter, I "met" my Soul, and at last I knew without a shadow of a doubt why I was on the planet. That was a transformational game-changer. *No programming degree required.*

THE CLARITY OF HINDSIGHT

What I can now see so clearly is that Imposter Syndrome caused me to lose sight of the truth: talent, hard work, and out-of-the-box thinking made it possible to achieve a level of success I never dreamed possible. I did that! My databases functioned beautifully and lasted. Some were still being updated and used daily fifteen years later. That's an accomplishment of which to be proud.

Sadly, in my moment of devastation, I was blinded to this truth. I could only see the darkness of that black hole and felt like I was falling into it. I wanted to run away from the pain and never look back.

Years later, one of my coaches helped me get clarity about how I ended up in such a backward, twisted knot. Reality outgrew my vision of self and bam! I slammed into the brick wall of full-blown Imposter Syndrome.

Oh, how effective we humans deceive and defeat ourselves. That's crazy, yet people do it to themselves every day. Now I recognize it as a form of self-torture, which I help clients recognize and overcome so they don't crash and burn.

During my healing journey, I discovered a powerful secret to making friends with Ego and forever banishing Impostor Syndrome and low self-esteem. It's worked for me and a great many others. That's the tool I'm excited to share with you now.

THE TOOL

Pow Wow With Three Aspects of Self is a guided visualization journey to meet with Ego, Higher Self, and Soul to promote balance and harmony within self. Humanity is presently evolving from an ego-centric to a soul-centered oneness of being. This tool was created to facilitate that process.

Your objective is to allow each aspect of self to have their say with the goal of negotiating a compromise. You may find they just want to be heard, or you may find they have some stipulations. There's no rush, and you don't want to force anything. Go with the flow, listen, and prepare to be flexible.

Ego isn't evil, nor is it your enemy. Ego is simply doing what it was tasked to do — keep you safe until you die. That mocking ego voice has prevented you from impetuously cutting your life short or incurring serious injury over a great many lifetimes. However, in this new, enlightened era, Ego is still keeping the brakes on while Soul hits the accelerator. It's time for Ego to back off and allow Soul to take the lead so that you might expand more fully into your purpose. This simple exercise will help you encourage that shift. It can be as long or short as you choose and can be repeated if needed.

Don't be surprised if the whole process flows with ease. I highly recommend setting your intention that it be so. This work is all about energy and intention.

What you'll need: A way to record your experience. You may speak it into a recorder, type it on an electronic device, or hand write. Choose what feels best to you but make it a point to record it in some way with as much detail as possible about what you see, feel, hear, and sense. This is a significant meeting, and you want to remember everything. Small details that seem insignificant in the moment may be important at a later date.

Preparation: Choose a quiet, comfortable place to sit. It can be indoors or outdoors. The important thing is that it be as free of distraction as possible.

Take your seat and settle into a comfortable position. You may want to shake out your arms and hands, flex your head and neck, allowing tightness held there to flow away.

Audio Recording: If you prefer to listen to an audio, you'll find one here: https://AkashaUnleashed.com/wu

Exercise Begins: When you're ready to begin, close your eyes and take three deep breaths. Breathe in as long as it feels comfortable; holding as long as it feels comfortable; exhaling as long as it feels comfortable. After the third exhale, begin breathing normally, putting your focus upon your breathing.

With each exhale, notice yourself slipping into a more deeply relaxed state while any tightness flows down your body and exits through your fingers and the bottoms of your feet. Take your time; there's no rush.

You'll notice your arms and hands feeling heavy, your breath steady and even.

In this deeply relaxed space, allow yourself to drift slowly up into and then out through your crown chakra (top of your head). As you move slightly higher, you'll find yourself (Soul), comfortably seated cross-legged in a triangular formation with Ego and higher self.

If they have not yet arrived, call upon them and invite them to join you. They should be there in short order. No judgments about what they look like. Allow them to present themselves in whatever way they wish.

Once the three of you are seated facing each other, welcome them warmly. You may engage in some preliminary friendly conversation or get right to the point. This is your journey, so do what feels best.

Be sure to take note of what they look like, what they're wearing, and any details you notice. Those details could be important to gleaning greater understanding later.

When you feel the lines of communication are open, turn your attention to Ego and inquire about Ego's needs and wants.

Repeat with Higher Self.

Having heard both of them out, explain Soul's position. They need to understand Soul is not being frivolous, but expanding into a higher frequency state of being, and their cooperation is vital to the process.

Your purpose is not to boss them around; you want to elicit their cooperation. Once they understand your why, they might surprise you with a willingness to work with you.

Continue the dialog until you are satisfied. Then respectfully thank them and promise to abide by whatever agreement you have made, asking them to do the same. You may choose to embrace them or not. Do what feels best to you.

When you're ready to return to present reality, allow yourself to float back down through your crown chakra and settle completely back into your body.

Take a couple of deep breaths, wiggle your fingers and toes, then when you're ready, open your eyes.

Welcome back to your new state of peace, balance, and harmony as a soul-centered being.

Debbra Lupien, Spiritual Teacher, and Voice of the Akashic Records, believes the most important question in life is: What feeds my Soul? When you figure that out and start doing it, you'll be unstoppable!

Her international #1, bestselling-book, *Akasha Unleashed: The Missing Manual To You*, has become a catalyst for personal transformations across the globe. Inspired by *Akasha Unleashed*, people seek Debbra out for guidance on their purpose and life journey.

Debbra spent decades seeking answers to the questions "Why am I here?" and "What am I supposed to accomplish?" After many false starts, she at last got her answers and, improbably, it was "all because of a horse."

Having found her passion and purpose, today Debbra's on fire to empower other women to get *their answers* so that they might create their unique version of happily ever after — with or without the prince.

When she's not exploring the halls of the Akashic Records, you may find Debbra at her mountaintop retreat with one husband, three horses, two crazy poodles, and a barn cat. She enjoys hiking, traveling, hanging out in the fifth dimension, and spontaneously bursting into song — because life's just that much fun!

https://www.thewellnessuniverse.com/world-changers/debbralupien/

CHAPTER 20

EMOTIONAL MASTERY

LEARNING LIFE'S LESSONS
TO CREATE AN AMAZING LIFE

by Ilene Dillon, MSW, LMFT, LCSW

MY STORY

Though I have always been an optimist and made the most of it, my childhood was miserable. Here are a few of the highlights:

- I was neglected for the first two years of my life, roaming my neighborhood naked and hungry, often taken in by the neighbors. It was enough for my father to be awarded custody of two little girls (my 4-year old sister and me, age 2) as a single father in 1945.

- My father removed us forcefully from our home, introduced us immediately to our "new mother," without explanation. Children were expected to be adaptable.

- I attended boarding schools during the week from age 2-4 ½, cared for on weekends by my father. I was born when he was stationed in New Guinea during World War II. I didn't know him when he came and took us away after giving my mother a bloody nose from his forceful slap.

- I taught myself to read when my sister started school so that I could be "with" her every day. She was the only constant mother figure I had ever known. As an infant, I attached to her. That attachment saved my life.

- I spent a year with my step-grandparents starting at five years old. It was the best year of my childhood, living on the farm and being healed by my grandparents' love, animals, and nature. The downside was that when I was returned home, nobody seemed to recall that I had been away, insisting I'd had experiences with them that I had not had. I felt terrible.

- My father was a career Air Force Officer. We moved every 18 months to three years. I went to 14 different schools before high school graduation. My father insisted we make A's and B's without concern for the different learning environments and curricula. Making friends was temporary because they (or we) moved away, and we never saw them again.

- As in many military families of the time, there was abuse—of many kinds--following the "A man's home is his castle" philosophy. If we got angry or cried, we were slapped until we stopped. This meant we learned to hold emotions inside.

When emotions are held inside, they grow. As a young adult, I was filled with anger and rage.

Is it any wonder that I married at the age of 19 and moved all the way across the country from my family? My young husband was also escaping a challenging family situation.

Together, we did a lot of healing. We both got into therapy and started healing emotional wounds. We learned to snow ski and backpack. We enjoyed being kids together. We got a lot of help from a couple who owned the houseboat dock we lived on, who helped us grow up and be more complete people. We worked and helped ourselves and each other through college and then graduate school. We were together nearly eight years before our daughter—whom we consciously conceived—was born. She was ten months old when my husband came home one day and announced he was moving out because he was not ready to be a father. I yelled at him, "What do you want me to do, send her back?"

When he left, a dam burst inside me. All the anger and hate and fury that had been growing inside of me since my beginning here on earth flooded out of me. I watched in horror as it dumped onto my precious little child.

Desperately, I started searching for what I needed to know or learn to keep from ruining my daughter's young life with the anger I could not stop. University Libraries (in those pre-Internet days) held NO answers. Educational institutions did not offer stand-alone classes on anger. There were no answers to, "Why do we have anger?" "What makes it so powerful?" "Can we get rid of it?" Or "Will it ever end?"

I sought answers everywhere. By then, I was a licensed marriage counselor, so I studied my clients, talked with my colleagues, and read whatever I could find (*Seth Speaks* and *The Nature of Personal Reality*, as well as professional books). I worked more through my psychotherapy. I joined a Spiritual Awareness Class and began to learn ancient spiritual principles onto which I could hold, such as *Energy follows attention* and *Whatever we pay attention to, we tend to become.*

After several years, I had answers to most of my questions. They began to fall together into an understanding of what emotions are (energy), what their purpose is (to help us learn lessons), and how to work with them (partner with them to hear and use their message). Not only did I become a *Recovered Angry Person* (at long, long last!), but I had developed a powerful way of working with all emotions. Eventually, I realized I was in charge of my emotional life. Emotions were no longer running me!

I started calling this state of being—the one where I was in charge of emotions, and they were no longer in charge of my life—Emotional Mastery.

It was so exciting that I started testing it out with clients who volunteered to experiment. I taught it in classes and through speeches. I incorporated it into the system of Parenting Consciously I developed as a single parent (make lemonade out of lemons) and was teaching in the US and around the world. Other people's lives started improving, too.

My "a-ha moment" took a long, laborious time to emerge, but it did! In 2019, I wrote and published my first book (*Emotions in Motion*). Now in publication is my second book, *Ending Manipulation*. Next year I'll be publishing *Turning Anger Into Enthusiasm*. I intend to write a book a year, and I have several books in mind.

In the year of this writing, I am turning 78. When my husband died four years previously, I decided to clear out and sell our home. I closed down my brick and mortar practice, closed down my internet radio program after 13 years, and bought a 24-foot recreational vehicle. In the following three years, I visited 31 US states and 4 Canadian provinces, writing, teaching, and making friends along the way. I'm now *Fear-less*. While we can't get rid of emotions (because they're energy and can't be created or destroyed), I can certainly reduce their presence and impact in my life. I now feel like I don't *do* fear; it comes up so seldom!

I'm a healthy and happy person, enjoying my life, and looking forward to quite a bit more of it. Part of my message to the world is this: No matter what happens in your life, when you learn to live from the *inside, out*, you can overcome the negative effects. In fact, *we're designed to heal ourselves and learn the lessons life brings us!*

It's exciting for me to be sharing with the world what I've learned, to help speed the healing and learning process of others. We can tap or meditate emotions away, but I advocate we work with emotions first, so we learn the lessons our experiences bring. And this we do best by living from the *inside, out.*

THE TOOL

Living From the *Inside, Out*

The secret to having your life flow smoothly and calmly, with you empowered and joyful, is to live it from the *inside, out.*

Living life from the *inside, out* is not actually a tool, *it's a total mindset change*. It requires an understanding of how life works and how you can work much more effectively with it than most of us have ever been taught to do.

Let's start by setting the scene.

Earth is a Giant School. All of us human beings have come here to learn and grow. We learn by having experiences. Each experience is an opportunity—an opportunity to learn and grow. We don't have to use the opportunity and learn the lesson, but a familiar yet curious thing happens if we don't.

Say your experience is that someone in your life acts disrespectfully to you. This doesn't feel good, of course, but since most of us don't like change and put it off as long as we can, you may not act definitively to end the disrespect. It happens once, and you think about putting a stop to it. But you postpone your action, not really wanting to hurt anyone or oust them from your life. It happens again, and again it feels painful to you. In fact, acts of disrespect occur in your life over and over again. Each time one is perpetrated, it's more painful. You might put off dealing with the disrespect in your life for months or even years. Your pain increases and increases. This is what happens when we've been presented with a lesson, and we avoid it or refuse to learn it. We all do this, tolerating uncomfortable, painful, and difficult situations rather than changing or ending them.

When the lessons of our experiences are not learned, they repeat and repeat—each time causing us more pain.

This is nature's way of motivating us to make change and grow. When we live from the *outside, in*, we think someone is picking on us, fate has it in for us, or something is wrong with us. In reality, we're just not learning the lesson that's been presented.

Emotions accompany our experiences. They are given to us as helpers, starting from the beginning of our life and staying with us 24/7/365 for our *entire lives!* They have to be important since they're with us for our total lives. Even if we develop Alzheimer's and aren't in the world cognitively, we still have emotions. They come up with our experiences because they have messages for us. When we decode and apply the message of an emotion, we can learn the lesson of our experiences. (See my book, *Emotions in Motion*, for the message of 12 common emotions.)

Do you want the good—actually the great—news? *The second we learn the lesson of our experience, that lesson is finished! It's over.* No more repetition of the experience or the pain. That lesson is complete. We get a break, then are presented with the next experience containing a lesson.

We're in a Giant School. We can follow our own pace in doing the learning, but the learning itself never stops.

When I discovered this, I concluded that learning the lesson presented by a particular experience was the *first thing* I wanted to do after I had the experience! I started embracing learning as soon as I could after an experience and learned something else important: the more you embrace learning here on the earth, the easier that learning becomes. Less pain, more gain!

HOW WE LEARN OUR LESSONS

It's actually pretty easy. We can just ask what we need to learn from a particular experience. We keep asking—and listening—and the answer will be given to us. Then we can use it to complete our learning.

Who do we ask? It depends upon what you believe. You can ask your Higher Mind, your Intuitive Self, a Saint, your Guides, or God (or another deity in whom you believe). It helps if it is an authority larger than yourself because it's easier to believe they can see and will know more. It really doesn't matter who you ask. But it does matter that you *do* ask, because of the principle that says *Help that isn't asked for, never works.* This means that if we don't ask for help, it won't be given. When we do ask for help, it's readily available.

I once was skiing at the top of Mt. Bachelor, a cone-shaped mountain in central Oregon. It was icy, and I fell. My ski clothing was slick, so I started spinning as I slipped down the mountain. I relaxed as fully as I could, but every time my feet were pointing down, I slammed the edges of my skis into the ice to see if I could stop myself. It didn't work. Ice chunks flew into the air, but the spinning didn't stop. I began to notice some huge boulders below me. I was heading straight for them. I started talking to God. "I need help, here, God. I do *not* want to hit my head on those rocks. Please help me to avoid those rocks." I didn't know what would happen, but I knew nothing could if I didn't ask. When I arrived in the area of the boulders, I slipped around them in such a way that I didn't hit my head—or any part of me. In fact, sliding a full third of the way down the mountain, I only injured one thumb, which happened when I arrived at last into softer snow and rolled over my own hand.

Ask.

Ask *What is it that I need to know from having this experience? I'm ready to learn whatever it takes. Please show me what I need to learn.* You might also want to ask: *What would I need to believe in order to have this experience?* We live life based on what we believe, and most of our beliefs are hidden from us, so this is a good way to find out what they are. Beliefs can be changed!

Keep asking as long as it takes until you get an answer. Listen to the answer. You may have to do a little decoding, or look into your past, or notice something you need to change. Use the message of the emotions that accompanied the experience and the answer you're given to unlock the puzzle and do the learning, so you learn and grow.

INSIDE, OUT

To do this well, you need to change your mindset. Instead of being in a world where others do things *to you,* where someone else is to blame, where *fate* has it in for you, or your parents didn't give you a good enough start in life, shift.

Shift to realizing that life works better when you live it from the *inside, out,* which means that you accept the notion that experiences you have are tailored to help you learn; that you can only change yourself, not anyone else. Realize that the only time you have the power to make change is in the present; that what you have inside of you, you tend to attract from outside. Our world operates like a mirror, with the people and experiences we have mirroring ourselves back to us. Accept that you, like every other person in the world—are individually responsible for your own life. You are a Co-Creator of your life, creating by what you pay attention to and through your beliefs, choices, and actions.

I used to steal—usually office supplies from my place of business. Something I learned in my childhood. Others also stole from me. When at last, I decided to stop stealing, my life changed drastically. Not only did people stop stealing from me or cheating me, people remembered to pay me money I had long forgotten about, sometimes with interest! My experience outside of me was mirroring who I was inside. I didn't steal, and nobody stole from me. It's just that simple.

If you stop judging yourself, others will soon stop judging you, too. And you'll stop judging others! When you focus on loving yourself and living by practicing love no matter what, you will be met with more love. Whatever you have inside of you will be reflected from outside of you.

It's because we are energy beings. These days, we're all becoming more aware of our energy nature. Emotions are energy. When we follow the message of the emotions we experience, life moves with greater ease.

Love says *come closer*. Loneliness says *bring more energy into yourself—love yourself more*. Fear says *unknown ahead—exercise caution and stay alert*. Jealousy says *get more creative and create what you want in your life*. Following these instructions *inside of ourselves and for ourselves*, changes our life forever.

Living life *inside, out*, proceeds this way.

1. You have an experience.

2. You feel emotions, such as anger, fear, or loneliness. You identify the message of the emotions.

3. You embrace the opportunity to learn by deciding to learn and asking for help.

4. You use the information you've gathered from the experience, the emotions, and the help to learn the lesson.

5. You give yourself permission to change and alter your beliefs, actions, or perceptions inside of yourself.

6. You feel what this change feels like.

7. You allow yourself to experience Gratitude—to yourself and for the lesson and help.

8. You rest, then move on.

I love *experiments*. Instead of asking yourself to change everything (the way we do with New Year's Resolutions), decide to experiment with your new learning or behavior—do it every day for at least three weeks. If you don't want to continue after the three weeks, change back.

At first, you may feel like all you do is learn lessons and make change. But keep it up, because once you learn to live from the *inside, out*, your entire experience of life will change for the better. You'll make lasting change, change which is able to take you happily and easily through the rest of your life.

Be Grateful.

The principle is this: *Gratitude is the Law of Increase. Whatever You Are Grateful for, You Will Get More Of.*

 Ilene Dillon, MSW, LMFT, LCSW, is a global Transformation Specialist who is changing human lives one mastered emotion at a time. A *Recovered Angry Person*, Ilene heads Emotional Mastery for Life. She offers international speaking, in-person and virtual workshops, and media for helping people become Emotional Masters, End Manipulation, Master Anger, and develop Fear-less living. She is the author of *Emotions in Motion: Mastering Life's Built-in Navigation System* and is publishing *Ending Manipulation*.

Still practicing (50 years) as a Marriage and Family Therapist and Clinical Social Worker to help people bring their lives back into harmony with spiritual principle, Ilene leads people to transform their lives from the *inside, out*, rediscovering and developing self-love, high self-esteem, happiness, and joy, smoothly and easily incorporating these in every aspect and relationship of their lives. A global speaker who frequently appears on summits and podcasts, Ilene offers tools and wisdom for living our best lives.

Ilene is birth mother of two and adoptive mother of one, with three adult stepdaughters. Her husband, neurosurgeon Dr. Robert Fink, died in 2016. In 2017, at the age of 74, Ilene closed down her brick and mortar businesses, sold their home, bought a 24 foot RV, and began roaming the US and Canada with her 8 pound Maltipoo dog, Pi. She incorporates into her own life what she teaches and no longer "does" fear, anger, depression, jealousy, loneliness, guilt, or shame.

https://www.thewellnessuniverse.com/world-changers/ilenedillon/

CHAPTER 21

EARTHING

CONNECT TO NATURE TO SOOTHE BODY, MIND, AND SOUL

by Jenine "J9" Mayring, CRM, CEMP, CCHP, CHT

MY STORY

The early morning sky was nearly dark. As the sun's rays began to slowly rise above the horizon, it brought the slightest bit of warmth to the chilly March morning. A slight wind rustled the desert brush. The air was crisp in the middle of Joshua Tree, California, but it was invigorating!

As I stood there, barefoot on the Earth, I was literally getting grounded while witnessing the magic of another day coming to life. This was my morning ritual for the 30 days that I lived out in the desert, which changed my life in the most profound way.

You see, being born and raised in Brooklyn, NYC, nature wasn't exactly right outside the front door (or stoop). However, I'm grateful that I was lucky enough to have had the privilege of going to our "country house" (as we city kids called it) on the weekends. It was there that my sisters, cousins, and I played in the green grass, adventured out into the woods, and frolicked at the beach on warm, summer days.

There were also occasional family trips to the Northeast, whether apple picking in upstate New York or camping in Vermont or the like. No matter the destination, getting out of the concrete jungle, and spending time in nature was like hitting the reset button. Stress melted away, and our creativity came back to life. Nature always seemed to restore a sort of calm for me as a kid.

One that I didn't quite fully grasp until that month I lived in the desert. Tuning in to the symphony of sounds and sights there brought a whole new level of expansion in consciousness. When I returned home to my 950 square-foot apartment, quite a drastic change of location, I had an epiphany.

I realized why I had felt drawn back to Brooklyn after living out west for over a decade. In an instant, the vision was clear. I was being called to create a sacred space for urbanites to reconnect to the healing properties of nature. To help my fellow New Yorkers rekindle that long-forgotten relationship with Mother Earth. To create a healing sanctuary that harnesses Earth elements to relieve stress and restore balance to the body, mind, and soul.

"To touch the earth is to have harmony with nature."

–Oglala Sioux

THE TOOL

No matter where your ancestors lived, most of them likely had a direct, physical connection to the Earth. Before urbanization, many of us lived on the land and grew our own food. It was a sustainable cycle that kept us balanced in many ways.

Nowadays, most of us are completely disconnected from our ancient roots. We live in a modern world with asphalt or pavement and rubber-soled shoes that quite literally separate us from our origins. We have been energetically cut off from the healing power of the planet. It's no wonder that as a society, we have become so stressed and out of alignment.

Wherever you happen to live in the world, there is a simple tool that you can easily incorporate into your daily routine to reduce stress and a plethora of other health benefits. It's called **Earthing**. Have you ever heard of it? Basically, it's the act of putting your bare feet in direct contact with the Earth to connect your body with the naturally balancing electric frequencies of the Earth. Sounds so simple, but when was the last time you actually did it?

*"The body is a highly intelligent electro-biochemical system that is strongly influenced by its internal electrical environment...
As I have learned through my research and that of my colleagues, contact with the surface of the Earth maintains the body's electrical stability and the normal functioning of its self-regulating and self-healing mechanisms.
The ground thus acts as the very same stabilizing resource for both the body and electrical systems throughout the world."*

– Gaétan Chevalier, Ph.D., Visiting Scientist, Developmental and Cell Biology Department, University of California at Irvine

THE PROBLEM

According to a national survey released by the American Psychological Association, one-third of Americans live with extreme stress, and nearly half of Americans (48 percent) believe that their stress has increased over the past five years. Both physical and psychological stress can contribute to health problems ranging from heart disease to obesity and fatigue, poor relationships, and decreased productivity. Therefore, any natural therapy for relieving stress has enormous potential to prevent or decrease the negative effects of most diseases.

THE SOLUTION: DECREASE STRESS NATURALLY

Since the 1990s, doctors and researchers have been pursuing scientific evidence to show that grounding, also known as Earthing, positively impacts human physiology and health. In multiple studies, Earthing has been documented to have a significant stress-reducing effect due to its systemic impact on the body, including the following:

- A normalizing influence on cortisol, the stress hormone.

- A calming impact on the electrical activity of the brain.

- A normalization of muscle tension.

- A rapid shift from a typically overactive sympathetic nervous system expression, associated with stress, into a parasympathetic, calming mode within the autonomic nervous system (ANS) that regulates heart and respiration rates, digestion, perspiration, urination, and even sexual arousal.

- Within the ANS, also an improvement of heart rate variability (HRV) – the miniscule variations in the heart's beat-to-beat interval – that serves as an accurate reflector of stress. Poor HRV is associated with stress-related disorders, cardiovascular disease, diabetes, mental health issues, and reduced lifespan. Grounding improves HRV to a degree far beyond mere relaxation.

Ref: 1, 2, 3, 4, 5

"In short, Earthing restores and maintains the human body's most natural electrical state, which in turn promotes optimum health and functionality in daily life. The primordial natural energy emanating from the Earth is the ultimate anti-inflammatory and the ultimate anti-aging medicine.

–James L. Oschman, Ph.D., Author of *Energy Medicine: The Scientific Basis* and *Energy Medicine in Therapeutics and Human Performance.*

Earthing is one of the easiest things you can do to improve your physical and mental health! So how do you do it? Just take off your shoes and socks, and put your bare feet on the ground (grass, dirt, sand, etc.). That's it! By establishing direct contact with the Earth's electron-rich surface, we quickly create electrical stability, which in turn heals physiological dysfunction and relieves stress.

More and more research is becoming available to support the healing benefits of grounding. In 2012, an informal experiment organized by Christy Westen, D.C., was conducted with 100 women in Southern California. After Earthing for only one hour, here are the results:

1. STRESS – 77 percent reported less stress, on average, about 50 percent better.

2. ENERGY – 78 percent reported more energy, on average, an increase of about 40 percent.

3. PAIN – 60 percent of those with pain said they had less pain at the end and an average decrease of about 30 percent.

4. MOOD – 82 percent said their mood had improved, with an average of 40 percent.

5. COMPLEXION – 73 percent thought they looked better, with an average improvement of 38 percent (the change was attributed to improved circulation and more calmness).

6. CIRCULATION – 65 percent stated that their circulation had improved, and on average, by 32 percent.

7. FLEXIBILITY – 62 percent reported improvement, with about a 23 percent improvement.

If you don't have easy access to the outdoors, some companies make grounding or Earthing mats, blankets, and even bed sheets. These items are plugged into the ground portion of a regular wall outlet. I sleep on an Earthing mat every night and also have an Earthing wristband for traveling. Easy to use and highly recommended. Say goodbye to jet lag!

In a study published in 2004, the participants provided feedback on their health issues before and after sleeping grounded for a period of eight weeks. The summary includes the following health benefits:

- Significant sense of well-being
- Reduced or eliminated inflammation
- Reduced or eliminated pain
- Reduced or eliminated fatigue
- Easier to fall asleep, sleeping much deeper, improved quality of sleep, feeling more rested, stopped snoring, no more nightmares
- Decreased PMS (premenstrual syndrome), menstrual periods not as severe, cramps not as strong, minimized food cravings, less depression

- Improved digestion, reduced gastrointestinal upset, less bloating, constipation, and nausea
- TMJ (temporomandibular joint disorder) significantly improved, ceased jaw clenching

If you're already familiar with Earthing, feel free to integrate your Earthing practice with meditation or visualization to take it to the next level. For example, I like to imagine energetic "roots" growing out of my soles and connecting into the center of the Earth's soul. Then I visualize deep red, soothing energy coming up into my feet, up my legs, and throughout my whole body, breathing in Mother Earth's nurturing energy into every cell of my being. Everything is energy, and energy can be mindfully focused by your intention.

Nature is an integral part of the fabric of the universe, which connects us all energetically. As a result, when you begin healing yourself, the entire collective consciousness begins to heal as well. So, remember to keep your feet on the ground and keep reaching for the stars!

"We are made from Mother Earth, and we go back to Mother Earth."

−Shenandoah

Jenine "J9" Mayring, CRM, CEMP, CCHP, CHT is widely known by her spiritual name, **Divine J9**. As a spiritual guide, best-selling author, international speaker, and award-winning writer, **Divine J9** leads soulful spiritual ceremonies as well as teaches workshops worldwide on mindfulness, meditation, spirituality, and personal growth. She lovingly reminds us that we are a product of what we feed ourselves daily, both mentally and physically, and provides simple solutions to align with our highest self.

Divine J9 is the founder of the alternative medicine healing sanctuary Body Mind Salt, the first and only wellness center of its kind to offer a wide range of complementary and alternative medicine modalities under one roof in Brooklyn, New York. She is deeply passionate about creating sacred space for healing the body-mind-soul.

Divine J9 is a certified shamanic energy medicine practitioner, certified Reiki master practitioner, certified crystal healing practitioner, certified hypnotherapist, certified professional speaker, ordained interfaith minister, certified wedding officiant, and registered NYC marriage officiant. She also holds honorary doctorate degrees in Metaphysics (Dr.Mph.) and Divinity (D.D.).

https://www.thewellnessuniverse.com/world-changers/divinej9/

References:

1. M. Ghaly and D. Teplitz, "The biologic effects of grounding the human body during sleep as measured by cortisol levels and subjective reporting of sleep, pain, and stress," Journal of Alternative and Complementary Medicine, vol. 10, no. 5, pp. 767–776, 2004.

2. G. Chevalier, K. Mori, and J. L. Oschman, "The effect of Earthing (grounding) on human physiology, Part I" European Biology and Bioelectromagnetics, vol. 2, no. 1, pp. 600–621, 2006.

3. G. Chevalier, "Changes in pulse rate, respiratory rate, blood oxygenation, perfusion index, skin conductance, and their variability induced during and after grounding human subjects for 40 minutes," Journal of Alternative and Complementary Medicine, vol. 16, no. 1, pp. 1–7, 2010.

4. G. Chevalier and S. Sinatra, "Emotional stress, heart rate variability, grounding, and improved autonomic tone: clinical applications," Integrative Medicine: A Clinician's Journal, vol. 10, no. 3, 2011.

5. L. Oschman, G. Chevalier, and A.C. Ober. "Biophysics of Earthing (Grounding) the Human Body" In Bioelectromagnetic and subtle energy medicine, 2nd Edition, P.J. Rosch Ed., CRC Press, New York, pp. 427-450, 2015.

CHAPTER 22

ReLAX!

FROM STRESS TO SERENITY IN SIXTEEN MINUTES!

by David D McLeod, DD, PhD, CMLC

MY STORY

Cruise control. 65 miles per hour. Six feet off the ground. Through the trees.

Not exactly textbook car handling technique! But that's where I found myself.

Moments earlier, I had been cruising homeward on Highway 280 in my sporty red Hyundai Sonata, listening to some great music from a local artist I had met in downtown San Carlos a couple of days before. It was about five o'clock, and I was just ten minutes away from my home, enjoying the warm afternoon sun and the minimal Sunday traffic when I started following a gentle curve to the left. I never completed the turn.

If you've ever driven a car for a prolonged distance, then you have probably had the experience of feeling yourself nodding off to sleep. On the rare occasion that it's happened to me, I've generally found myself quickly jerked awake by a jolt of adrenaline that pumps my alertness until I can stop my car and take a brief rest. Well, not this time!

I can't say for sure if I fell asleep at the wheel or not. What I can say is that I suddenly found myself in what seemed like an alien universe! I was completely disoriented. Time had slowed to a crawl. There was a loud surround-sound of *"Screee! Ch-ch-ch! Thwack! Ch-ch-ch-ch!"*

As I looked around, I recognized that I was still inside my car, but the only thing I could see beyond the vehicle itself was flickering shades of green and brown that slapped against the windows in time with the strange noises. *"Squeeeel! Ch-ch-ch! Whump!"*

What the—? I struggled to make sense of my situation, and it finally dawned on me that my car had left the road, and I was now hurtling through trees and bushes. At my original freeway speed!

As the truth finally blossomed in my mind, a fist of fear clutched at my heart. I could feel cold steel panic erupting from my gut, and my body started to tense up in preparation for the worst.

All of a sudden, the car filled with the sound of a powerful, deep voice that roared one slow word: **"REEEELAAAAAX!"** I have no idea where this sound came from, but it seemed to exist everywhere simultaneously. Since everything appeared to be happening in slow motion, I paused and considered my options:

1. Panic: *C'mon, dude!! Stop messin' around! Grab the wheel, hit those brakes, and wrestle this beast to a halt.*

2. Reason: *This might be a good time to pay attention to, you know, the BIG VOICE out there...*

3. Uncertainty: *Hey, don't look at me! You outta options, boy! Better choose fast!*

Since external visibility had dropped to near zero, option one was out of the question, so I said out loud, "Okay, I dunno who you are, but you're right. Sensible thing here is to do my best to relax and just wait for this ride to end."

I gasped deeply, closed my eyes, and released my hands into my lap. "Okay," I said, "It's all up to you now."

Instantly, we were back in real-time. The car was thrashing through the trees now. I felt smacks and bumps as the vehicle shifted left and right; I saw flashes of light as branches and leaves clawed at the windshield, and soon gave way to open air. The side airbag exploded with a loud *"Bang!"* over my left ear. And then, a final *"Wham!"* that caused me to slump down in my seat and the car came to a stop.

Without thinking, I reached over and turned off the still-running engine. And then I did a quick survey.

No blood or guts anywhere. No immediate pain. No apparent broken bones. *Whew!*

The front windshield had cracked in multiple places but had miraculously not shattered. Debris littered the inside of the car—obviously the result of driving with the sunroof open—but most of that was just leaves and branches.

Neither of the doors would open. It appeared my only way out was through the sunroof. I twisted around and fumbled my way to an awkward standing position. My feet straddled the center console as I poked my head out. When I was fully upright, I looked toward the rear of the car, and I was stunned by what I saw.

About 20 yards back stood two hefty oak trees approximately six feet apart. Each tree-trunk had a vertical white stripe where the bark had been scraped away. *Holy Shit!*, I thought. My eyes popped, and my jaw dropped as I realized that these 18-inch gashes started about five to six feet above ground level. I was jolted by a sudden surge of intense emotion at the realization that I had actually flown through the trees, to be grabbed in mid-air by these two oaks that quite literally held me long enough to slow me down and drop me to the ground.

I blinked and shook my head. *If I had been only an inch to either side…* The thought trailed away as I realized I would probably not be standing on this seat right now.

Tears leaped out of my head; convulsive sobs shook my body. A weird combination of fear, anger, sadness, and joy coursed through me all at the same time. As the intensity of this emotional energy diminished, it gave way to a profound sense of gratitude, the depth of which I had never experienced before.

After my body settled down and I regained my composure, I grabbed my backpack and cellphone, and I hopped out onto the soft, leafy underbrush.

My car had come to rest on a stretch of ground between the freeway and a parallel community roadway. Cars and bicycles moved lazily on the road, seemingly unaware that I had made this unscheduled stop. After I scrambled over a fence and shuffled to the service road—marveling once again that I could walk and move without pain—I stole a look back and understood immediately why no-one had approached: from the road, the car was practically invisible through the bushes!

I called 911 and explained the situation as best I could, and soon enough, I was joined by an EMT team who gave me a quick once-over inspection. A few minutes later, a tow-truck showed up, and the messy wreckage was quickly winched out of the bushes.

My poor Sonata—with less than 6,000 miles on the odometer—was clearly way beyond repair, but it still had to be taken to a registered body shop to be properly inspected and officially written off. I got the address of the garage and then made a second call to a friend who lived nearby.

Bob arrived just as the remains of the vehicle were being dragged onto the truck bed. He gawked at the debris and looked at me with his mouth wide open. Shaking his head, he whispered incredulously, "You walked away from that?!" He hugged me in his usual bear-like way, stepped back, looked at me sideways, and motioned to get into his van.

The drive to the hospital was silent for all of three minutes. Then Bob could no longer contain his curiosity, and questions just poured out of him. I still hadn't fully grasped my own understanding of the crash, but I shared what I could remember. He listened in disbelief.

At last, we made it to the hospital. After a short wait in the emergency room, I was thoroughly examined by a courteous, overworked doctor who assured me that I had suffered no more than superficial injuries.

RELUCTANT LESSONS

This was the second time I had been involved in a serious car accident where I had been driving, so obviously, the primary take-away from this particular crash was *Stay alert and drive more carefully!* But as I contemplated this dramatic incident over the following days and weeks, I became aware of a few other key lessons that have definitely shaped and influenced my life since that fateful moment at 5:00 pm on August 11, 2013.

The fact that I had walked away from a potentially fatal crash with only minor injuries was an unmistakable sign that this world was not quite done with me. At the same time, *Spirit-God-The Universe-Supreme Consciousness* (whatever you prefer) was clearly trying to get my attention. Apparently, subtle messages had failed to register, so something extreme had become necessary. Threading a vehicle at 65 mph between a pair of thick oak goalposts certainly filled the bill as an unforgettable wake-up call! The fact that I had nodded off behind the wheel without my typical knee-jerk response—almost as if I'd been induced into a state of temporary numbness—was just icing on the cake to make the event more dramatic and memorable for me.

Indeed, driving in cruise control while unconscious seemed an apt metaphor for my entire life! I had been allowing life to happen to me without making any inspired decisions or sharing any of the important life-lessons that I had already learned. On top of that, the fact that my low-flying vehicle was slowed to a stop by two perfectly positioned trees—something that could hardly have happened by random chance in a million years—led me to appreciate that some invisible force was truly looking after my life and providing guidance that I hadn't acknowledged before.

Over the next couple of weeks, I began to experience painful tension in my jaw and between my shoulder blades. Since the doctor had already confirmed that there was nothing physically wrong with me, it seemed likely that I was suffering the equivalent of intense post-traumatic stress. While I found some relief from Ibuprofen and Acetaminophen, I kept remembering that powerful, deep, booming voice, the one that had commanded me to **"RELAX!"** during my flight through the trees. It reminded me of a Yoga retreat I had attended in 2006; one of the teachers had used that same command in a very clever and structured way to encourage deep relaxation during the final portion of his class. While I was already a pretty dedicated Yoga practitioner by this time, I hadn't been doing the relaxation practice the way I had learned at that retreat. Given my current level of tension and pain, now seemed like a perfect time to revive that practice!

THE TOOL

THE *ReLAX!* PROCESS

OVERVIEW OF STRESS

In very simple terms, stress is a reaction to perceived pressure from some external situation or event. The reaction can be purely physical, like when your body is traumatized in some way, such as during a car accident. This form of stress may need to be healed through medical procedures or physical therapy, depending on the severity of the trauma. But for less serious forms of physical injury, simple relaxation techniques may prove effective.

The more insidious (and potentially more dangerous) form of stress, however, is generally of a mental or emotional nature. Common causes of this kind of stress include things like the loss of a job, the end of a marriage, illness or death of a family member, or serious financial problems.

When stress becomes chronic or overly intense, it can do actual damage to you, both mentally and physically. Prolonged stress can result in increased blood pressure, headaches, sleep challenges, digestive issues, reduced sex drive, not to mention moodiness, anxiety, and even depression. Often, emotional and mental stress is accompanied by significant muscular tension that manifests in a particular part of your body. In my case, this happens to be my jaw and shoulder muscles, but it can be anywhere.

As I have continued to study human psychology, particularly in the area of psychic shadow, what I've learned is that unconscious fear plays a big part in the stress reaction. This makes perfect sense if you think about it. When an external event happens, we can dispassionately see it as just another event, if we choose. But often, the event has a direct impact on our lives, and this can lead us into unconscious self-talk about the potential negative effects of that event, which causes our level of fear to rise. This, in turn, elevates our level of stress and all the effects that it can create. Most of the stress that people tend to experience is of this type.

The best way I've found to reduce stress in my life is by maximizing awareness of the unconscious fear that might be driving it. And to do that, I focus first on the physical tension itself. By reducing the tension, I find it easier to recognize the hidden fear I've been trying to avoid. When I see the fear itself, it almost always turns out to be an irrational fear with little or no basis in reality. A little laughter, acceptance, and gratitude help me to dissolve that fear quickly. And *voilà!* Immediate stress relief!

PROCESS PREPARATION

If you have done any Yoga, I'm sure you've been exposed to what must surely be the universal favorite pose: *Shavasana*. It is a simple pose that is widely used in Yoga because of its inherent ability to induce maximum relaxation.

Find a quiet place where you will not be disturbed for about 20 minutes and place a Yoga mat on the center of the floor. Lie down on the mat flat on your back with your legs shoulder-width apart and your arms at about a 30-degree angle from your body. Keep your hands arranged palms facing upward, and allow your feet to flop outward to the sides. Position your head to keep your neck as straight as possible relative to your spine and allow your body to sink into the floor beneath you.

Allow your eyes to close gently and begin to breathe slowly and deeply. With each slow inhale, imagine you are saying the words *"I Am"*. And then, as you slowly exhale, imagine you are saying the word *"Relaxed"*. Inhale, *"I Am"* Exhale, *"Relaxed"*. Repeat this for at least 10-12 repetitions, and with each cycle, feel yourself getting deeper and deeper into relaxation while remaining fully aware and awake.

PART 1: RE-TENSE AND RE-LEASE

You are now going to completely relax as many muscles as possible in your body. Start at your feet and work progressively toward your head. The idea is to bring maximum tension to a single muscle group and then to release it fully. While doing this, try to stay relaxed everywhere else in your body.

Start with your toes: Tighten the toes in both feet, and simultaneously take a very slow deep breath in as if you were sucking all that tension into your lungs. Then, simultaneously release the toes and expel all the air from your lungs, and say the word *"Re-Lease"*. Repeat this three times.

Move up to your calves: Tighten the calves in both legs (while keeping the rest of your body totally relaxed), and simultaneously inhale all the tension into your lungs. Then, simultaneously release the calf muscles and expel all the air from your lungs, and say the word *"Re-Lease"*. Repeat this three times.

Continue in this manner for every major muscle group in your body: quads, hamstrings, buttocks, lower back, stomach, chest, hands, biceps, triceps, shoulders, neck, jaw, and mouth. Perform extra *Re-Tense & Re-Lease* cycles for any area of your body that seems to need more attention.

When you are done, consciously release your body to the floor and take several more deep breaths until your breathing softens back to normal.

PART 2: LAUGH, ACCEPT, EXPRESS

Laugh: While still in the prone position, allow yourself to laugh out loud for at least a minute. Let the laughter start out in whatever way it will, but soon enough, you will begin to feel the energy, and it will become genuine and full-bodied. Continue as long as you can, and then let the laughter fade away. Calm your breath and regain your relaxed state. Gently lift yourself into a comfortable sitting position with your hands in your lap and your eyes gently closed.

Accept: Recognize that in this beautiful moment, everything about your life is perfect. Whatever fear may be present, simply accept it and allow it to pass through you. No matter what might be happening in your life, remember that you have handled everything the Universe has delivered so far—you have been 100% successful! So, be willing to accept what is and know that you will make your way through this too.

eXpress: Release any remaining fear from your body, and express total gratitude for every aspect of your life, recognizing that everything has come to you at your own invitation. Welcome it as a gift that is here to empower you to express and experience the fullness of who you really are—in every moment!

FINAL WORDS

Remember that you are the master of every aspect of your life, and you are always at choice. When things seem too big to carry, you can let stress overwhelm you, or you can **ReLAX!** Choose the latter for improved health and happiness.

Oh, yes, and remember to smile as you wrap yourself in a juicy, delicious hug of self-love!

Fighter pilot. Author. Software engineer. Mentor. Aerobics instructor. Poet. Janitor. Lifeguard. Musician. Radio host. Graphics designer. Father. Student. Teacher. Photographer. Ordained minister. Yogi.

These roles—and many others—add up to a LOT of life experience, which David McLeod brings to bear in his capacity as a transformational speaker, life-mastery coach, experiential facilitator, and writer/storyteller.

As a Certified Master Life Coach with a PhD in Holistic Life Coaching and a DD in Spiritual Counseling, David creates and shares powerful *Life Mastery Tools* that enable adult men and women to transcend triggers, challenges, and obstacles so that they can express and experience the fullness of who they really are and thereby manifest truly magnificent and fulfilling lives.

Connect with David at:

https://www.thewellnessuniverse.com/world-changers/davidmcleod/

CHAPTER 23

RECLAIMING YOUR POWER

SHINE SO BRIGHT
IT HURTS TO LOOK AT YOU

by Suzy Woo, B.Msc.

MY STORY

"You'll never amount to anything!"

"No one else would ever want you! Everyone is laughing at you. You're nothing without me!"

Sad face.

Sad heart.

Day in and day out, I felt myself slipping away as I became out of sight and out of mind to family and friends. I became isolated from society and insulated in a cocoon of toxicity, gas-lighting, substance abuse, and, eventually, full-blown domestic violence.

My prom date, who I viewed as my knight in shining armor, would be the same person who nearly killed me.

Would I really be nothing without him? Am I really worthless?

What the hell happened? Where did I go?

Who did I use to be? I was a bright, happy-go-lucky, empathic little girl who always had a smile on her face. I was a friend to the friendless and cheered people up. I got in the face of bullies when I saw someone being wronged, but I never stood up for myself.

By the age of nineteen, I was losing my shine. By twenty-five, I lost my spark. I lost my fuel. By thirty-five, I lost hope. I gave up on myself, certain that I would die at the hands of the very person who said he loved me the most.

I had left three times but reconciled, then we married. We had three children together.

Completely consumed by my fears, I lived in this dysfunctional state for a total of twenty-two years. I was like a zombie, dead inside.

Choose yourself sooner rather than later. Choose yourself now.

It took an earth-shattering crisis for me to take action to save myself. Why? I was not living in alignment with my purpose and relinquished my power.

Our loving universe sends us all kinds of signs, symbols, and synchronistic moments to help us get back on our path, including through other people.

When we don't listen, when we don't take corrective action, the consequences become far more devastating.

One morning, we were racing about getting ready for school and work when our 16-year old daughter pulled me aside. She looked me square in the eye and said, "I can't take living like this anymore. It's either him or me."

I went numb. Terrified inside, I knew she was right. There was no way I could let her go. I could never live with myself.

We made a pact that the next time he started flipping out, she would call 911.

It happened in less than two weeks, and my then-husband was arrested. Three months later, the kids and I moved to a new house.

I can vividly recall the first time waking up in my new bedroom. It was a privilege to have had slept all night without being assaulted. I opened my eyes to receive the most brilliant, picturesque, and warming sunrise I'd ever experienced. Deep, rich violets and creamy rose hues. The cheery intense yellows begged me to expand into my new found freedom. I couldn't help sobbing in humility. I was getting a message that this was a gift; to feel the hope of this new day and embrace this new lease on life. I was okay, I was alive, and I made it!

The road to emotional recovery was hard. I suffered from PTSD and had night terrors. Anger replaced my sadness and anxiety. I entered blame mode, big time. I blamed the world, blamed the ex, and here I sat, mad, stagnant, broke, and lost.

How could I have taken this from bad to worse? Alcohol. I drank at night to escape.

A few months later, I lost my job. My boss said I "just wasn't there anymore."

The unpaid bills piled up. I became resentful to the world. Unable to pay my car insurance, I had to take my vehicle off the road. I sold my antique kitchen set to keep my utilities on. I was sinking hard and fast.

Once you hit the bottom, you can't fall off the floor.

A caterpillar spends his life eating. He spins into a cocoon and then completely melts down into a pool of enzymes. If you split open the cocoon at the right time, it would be liquefied goo. That goo has everything it needs to reconstitute and emerge as a butterfly. A caterpillar cannot become fully transformed into its higher expression without first falling apart.

When we have repeating undesirable outcomes, we have to face that it can't always be everybody else's fault.

When we finally admit there is a problem, we may desperately lash out to pin the blame on others to deflect and protect our ego.

Once we can be blatantly honest with ourselves, we enter the goo stage, surrender. We dumpster-dive the depths of the stories we tell ourselves. We sift through the shipwrecked parts of ourselves, in search of the source of the belief system where the painful triggers stemmed from.

Our frames of reference become a blur, and we bottom out. We have a meltdown. This can also be called the dark night of the soul. It's a painful-but-necessary surrender. This confusing stage can last an hour, a week, or even a year.

It is crucial to be gentle with ourselves. We are being prepared to transform.

I remember waking up one morning feeling like the weight of the world was pinning me down. I begrudgingly said under my breath, "Ugh, I wonder what is going to happen to me today."

I stepped out of the side door to receive a stack of overdue bills from the mailman. I demanded, "Why don't you ever bring my anything good?"

My mailman was a calm, cool, down to earth guy in his thirties. He looked at me, and very matter-of-factly replied, "Buy something."

I half-chuckled and went back into the house.

It was an epiphany. He was absolutely right.

In that moment, everything shifted.

The world had collapsed around me, and up to this point, I had been waiting for some unknown force to rescue me, to fix and rebuild my life, to do the work for me. There I was again, giving my power away.

My victimhood mindset blamed the world for the lack in my life. When we point a finger of judgment, there are three more pointing back at us.

If we never apply for a job, we won't get an offer. If we're not at the bus stop, we obviously can't catch the bus. We must take positive action to create and manifest the path of our greatest desires. We must make a conscious decision to become fully accountable and take the reins to our lives.

Claiming ownership for my abusive marriage was the toughest pill to swallow. I confused acceptance with condoning. I needed to stake my claim and admit that regardless of my why, it was still a choice. Every time I chose to stay, I was not choosing my higher calling, and the consequences became much deeper and more serious.

Excited at my new perspective, thanks to the mailman, I headed to my desk, pulled together a plan, and within a week, launched my own IT services business, which quickly became successful.

I started to expect great things to happen. From this new vantage point, I woke up excited each day, saying, "What can I bring to this day!?" I looked for the amazing things, and they showed up.

THE TOOL

- Be cognizant of your thoughts! If we look for the crap in life, we will notice what's wrong and talk ourselves out of even trying. If we look for the best, we will notice opportunities.

- Once we claim ownership, we get a new, healthier, upgraded point of reference, and true healing can begin! We sweep up the chards of past pains; we hug the broken pieces of ourselves back together with unconditional love. No one else can do this for us.

- Take time for self-care. Release the past and become present. No more looking back, you don't live there anymore. You aren't the same person you were yesterday, or a week, a year, or a decade ago. Be here now.

- Find reasons to be grateful. You might have to dig at first. Name them. Think about how amazing life is. Thank your heart for beating for you, thank your feet for carrying you. Thank your breath, the oxygen, the trees, the gifts of this earth.

- Understand that you are a miracle! You are divine. You are made from the same ingredients as the entire universe. Who are you to talk down to divinity? Straighten your crown and embrace your creator energy. You are abundance, you are love, and you are loved.

- When you choose the people and situations that support your purpose, you will be rewarded with manifestation and joy. When we are living in the flow of creation and abundance, which again, is the exact frequency we are made of, everything that tries to hurt us merely falls away; because we do not allow it to have any power over us.

- Look for the lessons in everything and everyone. That lesson might be, "I never want to be like that person!" It may be, "Wow, that person inspires me to be more positive!"

- Think about a person whose presence lights up a room. We are all born with that inner light. Where is yours? Have you dimmed it because others have complained you are too bright, too loud, too weird, too different? Those people are asking you to change who you are. Regardless of their title, they are not your vibe, so don't include them in your tribe. Respect and love yourself enough to walk away.

- Be your own, authentic, unique divine expression. Shine bright like the sun in your own unique divine way. No one can turn off the sun. Shine so bright that it hurts to look at you!

Twelve businesses later, I am deeply in love with life as a spiritual healer, astrologer, and psychic medium, and spiritual and metaphysical shop owner. Before even opening my doors, I received an offer to open a second location. In the flow. I never get angry and my kids will tell you, I even laugh in my sleep.

- Love yourself fully. The world will meet you exactly where you are, but you must take positive actions to support your growth. Don't wait for anyone or anything outside of yourself.

- You are never alone. You are part of a loving, living breathing universe. You have an infinite spirit team!

- Smile more. Let go. Live a life that you love. Ditch expectations. Live fully.

- Take charge, crank your light and let nothing dim it, ever.

Thank you for allowing these words to speak to you.

In gratitude, I love you deeply and universally.

Here is a nice little meditative exercise I'll leave you with:

Get comfy, and close your eyes. Pay attention to your breath as you breathe deeply into the pit of your stomach. Visualize breathing out soot and pollution. Blow it out like birthday candles. Repeat this two more times, really blowing out everything toxic.

Now notice the sun, smiling at you. See the sun opening its arms and hugging you by showering you with it's warm, life-giving sun rays and light energy.

Feel the warmth on your skin and smile. Feel your skin absorbing the light energy. Begin to breathe in this beautiful golden frequency, allowing it to fill your throat, lungs, and your entire insides. Feel your cells drinking in this abundant, magnificent liquid light. Feel yourself radiating this sunlight energy.

Imagine your body's gas tank becoming filled with vitality, happiness, power, strength, and confidence. Smile as you receive this healing energy, allowing it to spill outside of your physical body and create a golden egg around you. Breathe this incredible sun energy. Hang out and enjoy this experience as long as you like. Seal it in like tying a balloon.

Give thanks from your heart and close the session.

What was your favorite tip or takeaway? I would love to hear from you!

Rev. Suzy Woo, B.Msc, is a spiritual healer, astrologer, psychic medium, author, and owner of Good for the Spirit Gifts, with a private healing practice in Orchard Park, New York. She uses a blending of modalities to heal past life, generational, and inner child trauma. She removes energetic imbalances and implants to promote healing on all layers.

Suzy loves motivational speaking and teaching workshops about crystals, astrology, mediumship, and zero-point energy to help people understand and connect with their own spiritual aspirations and talents. She is emphatic about her ever-growing crystal collection and is a crystal skull practitioner. Sharing the stage has always been a priority for Suzy; she has hosted (and will continue to host) several events, radio shows, and a television show where she features artisans and practitioners to share their passions.

Miniatures have always captivated Suzy since she was young. She paints and creates spiritual art with great detail.

After escaping 22 years of marital, domestic violence, she is a strong advocate for self-love and self-empowerment. She is the mom and biggest fan of three creative, kind, and entertaining humans; two dogs, two cats, two birds, two African dwarf frogs, and tropical fish.

https://www.thewellnessuniverse.com/world-changers/suzywoo/

CHAPTER 24

FORGIVENESS

HOW TO TRANSCEND RESENTMENT AND LIVE IN PEACE

by Elizabeth Kipp

MY STORY

How does an act of kindness turn into resentment and a grudge? It is a strange thing when an agreement is not honored, and the energy from that hurt turns to anger and resentment. When I felt victimized, collapsing into my sense of being devalued by close family member, my anger and righteous indignation propelled me into a false sense of power. It was a potent emotion and was amplified by the story I was telling myself: *How dare they betray me like this!* I did not know how to resolve this situation. And so, this unhealed wound festered into a full-on grudge.

Let me tell you my story.

A close family member was starting a business and asked me for a loan. I agreed because I felt confident in the venture and was sure that I would be repaid. We drew up legal papers for the loan, and we signed it with the commitment that once I loaned the money, I would be paid back in monthly increments for a number of years, including the current interest rate at the time. I loaned the money. I was so excited. This seemed like a win for both of us—the money needed to fuel a new business, and I would be repaid the principal with some interest added to it.

I received three monthly payments, and then the payments stopped. When I asked my relative what was happening, I received verbal assurances that the payments would commence. No further payments came. I did everything I knew the best I could, including acting on the recourse in the loan papers that detailed the consequences of missed payments, including cessation of the payments altogether. Still, I did not get repaid any further.

At first, I felt surprised. Then I felt disappointed. And then, as I realized I was not going to be repaid, I felt hurt and victimized. I turned the energy of this experience into and against myself as I asked myself: *How could you have so misjudged this?* And: *How could you be so stupid?*

But the energy of the experience had a momentum all its own. The hurt transformed into anger: at me and then toward the person to whom I had made the loan. My feelings went from hurt to feeling betrayed and personally transgressed. I was mad at the person, at myself, at the whole situation, and even at the world.

The only way I knew to deal with this whole situation was to deny how badly I felt. *It can't be all that bad*, I would tell myself when I felt my resentment rise as sensation in my body. As time went on, somehow, I unconsciously buried the wound of this experience. But it did not go away. For ten years, it festered and grew like a crystal inside me. On a conscious level, I went on with my life. I was estranged from the family member except for the cordial season's greetings exchange every year at Christmas. I did not like it, but I did not know how to repair the damage done. And I could not see a way to change my point of view. I felt completely justified in my stance on the matter: *We had an agreement. I trusted that you would honor the agreement. You broke that agreement, and in doing so, you dishonored me. I see that in your eyes I am not worth the effort to make good on the promise between us.*

How do you forgive when you are filled with resentment and righteous indignation? This question sat deep inside me for years.

It is not like I had any role models for dealing with such hurt. As a child, the people around me either denied their anger or expressed it so vehemently that its expression inflicted trauma on all those present when it was loosed. I was so traumatized by the effects of anger projected at me growing up that I withstood them the best that I could and vowed that I would never inflict or cast anger onto anyone in my life. I did the best I could to live up to that vow. When this loan debacle happened, I did not express my anger because I did not know how to do so in a healthy way. I learned later that pain continues to move through families until someone has the courage to feel it. Denying one's experience and moving forward as if nothing at all had happened was a way of life in the culture in which I was raised.

One day, ten years after the loan began, I was quietly working at my desk, and I realized that in my anger, I was holding a grudge. It seemed to me that I was receiving Divine guidance showing me what I had been doing all this time. I knew right away how unhealthy this was for myself and my relative. I felt a shift of energy inside me right away. It felt like a softening and an opening in my heart.

I had been holding onto intense negative energy, which was detrimental to me. And because of my righteous indignation, I was projecting the same negativity towards this person, which was injurious to them, too, energetically speaking. I saw right then that I needed to forgive my relative for what they had done. I was clear in my intention. I was not condoning what they had done. I was forgiving the trespass. I was releasing the pent-up energy inside me that felt betrayed. I felt another shift inside me. It felt as if a part of me opened and expanded. The expansion transmuted into compassion: for me, for the relative, for all we had been through because of this unfinished business.

As I sat in silent contemplation, I felt a sense of liberation. I was grateful to finally have been granted the awareness of seeing the depth to which my resentment had taken me. I felt blessed to finally be able to process and heal the pain I had carried for so long because of what had happened. And I felt a sense of peace.

I did not tell anyone about my experience of forgiveness at this time. It felt like a sacred and personal revelation. The most extraordinary thing happened three days later. My relative called me on the phone, and as if nothing had ever been tenuous between us, to let me know that he had sent me a payment. He spoke of his obligation to me.

I was more than a little pleasantly surprised. I had not said one word to this person about my forgiveness work. Yet this revealed that the metaphorical ice dam between us had broken. We remain good friends today. Forgiveness, true forgiveness, works like that.

I finally forgave both the other and myself. I could not change the past, but in the present moment, I could shift my prospects for the future. I discovered the toxic power and weight of carrying resentment. I managed to find forgiveness before things went too far, and I had lost myself forever. I had to find a way to redeem my soul and live with myself again. At the end of my search, I found ease and serenity.

THE TOOL

THE WHY AND HOW OF FORGIVENESS

THE WHY

You have an event in your life that shakes you to the core. You feel powerless and helpless to do anything about it. You are filled to the brim with feelings that leave you exceedingly uncomfortable in your skin. You want to find the valve to release the pressure, but you're not sure where it is or how to implement it when you find it. You want to escape, but does hitting the escape button really serve to heal, or hinder?

I understand. When such challenges in life come my way, a part of me wants to run away. A part of me wants to just crawl in a hole somewhere, shutdown, and disappear, or find solace in some distraction, or numb my feelings; to block out the whole thing. I see myself wanting to look away. I could engage in all manner of "what-ifs" and "why-did-this-happen" and driven myself right into serious illness myself with such negativity and insistence on holding on.

We can be aware of these patterns of avoidance or escapism as a coping mechanism. We can decide, instead of turning away from the hurt or wrong we have experienced, to turn toward healing this negative spiral of feeling so victimized by events we are powerless to change.

We do not have to sit in suffering. We can allow ourselves to feel what is coming up for us, but not allow ourselves to be gobbled up from the inside out by anger and resentment. We can make peace. We can learn to let go (more of an art than a science for me.) Forgiveness, letting go, is more of a process, a shift in perspective, rather than a sequence of discreetly measured steps to follow, and then it's complete.

THE HOW

The first step in letting go is presence.

We need presence to face our place of resistance around the hurt we experienced and allow ourselves to feel where it is expressing itself as sensation in the body.

Strive to understand the meaning we are making of what happened.

We cannot change what happened, but we can shift our perspective on what we believe about this event.

Accept our humanness.

Anger and frustration are all part of the human experience. Everyone feels these emotions. There is no shame in this. Instead of feeling as if we are in a dueling match with these qualities, we can turn into and accept what we are feeling. We learn to know these feelings intimately and accept them as an integral part of who we are. We deepen into self-compassion. Once we accept that we have these feelings, we come to a place of peace with them.

Become willing to forgive.

The beginning of forgiveness is being willing to let go of whatever it was that we are grasping onto so tightly around the hurt or wrong done to us.

Ask for help from a Higher Authority.

The word "forgive' comes from the words 'to forgo or forget.' We might be able to forgive someone intellectually, but if we do not remove the emotional charge around this event that we are forgiving, then we have not fully forgiven. We are not saying we're condoning what we are forgiving. We are saying fully forgiving. We might say, "I forgive, but I'll never forget."

By forgetting, we are always going to protect ourselves from being hurt like this again; hence we are unwilling to let this incident go altogether. This is not true and full forgiveness.

If you are having difficulty truly forgiving, what do you do? Where do you turn? You turn to a power greater than yourself to help you make this difficult step because you do not want this event to stay stuck within you. You may not have found a way to let it go by yourself. You ask, "Higher Power, all that You are, help me forgive all the events around this situation, no matter what. Help everyone involved in this situation to forgive me, and help us to forgive ourselves, completely and totally. Please, and thank You." As you say this, you might notice a release of energy in your body. The emotional charge that is built up inside of the body dissipates. By asking for help, the Higher Power grants your transcendence through this block of resentment towards what happened. True forgiveness lies in being able to release what is inside your physiology around the hurt or wrong you experienced. Otherwise, you are not addressing the core of the problem, and it will re-emerge.

We ask a Higher Power to help us forgive ourselves. If there are those we cannot forgive, we pray for them and send them a blessing.

Drop judgments about the situation.

Move from a position of feeling so much negativity to one of neutrality and objectivity. Here again, you can turn to a Higher Power of your understanding for help.

Let go of the fear of uncertainty.

The most important teacher lives within you. Remember and honor your worth and own your power.

Live in the present.

Stop daydreaming about the past and come into the present.

RESOLUTION, LIBERATION, AND PEACE

Because of the unresolved resentment I held, I had hidden away a part of myself. I was finally able to face the anger and the hurt I had felt and accepted it rather than deny it. I was able to integrate this lost part of me with love and compassion. Knowing myself through self-honesty and a willingness to see things from a new perspective, all served to help me transmute my pain into forgiveness. I stopped fighting myself and started working with myself.

Forgiveness is a quiet, private journey one takes deep down, where we feel our wounds the most, and into that place where we feel the loving energy of the Infinite. It is not on the outside, not a spiritual bypass, spoken with the pretense of proving we are bigger or more evolved, or more kind or loving. It is a personal walk to the core of our being where we forgive the source of the hurts we feel and grow the courage in our hearts to let them go and live free from their burden.

I finally forgave both the other and myself. You can do this, too. It takes presence, honesty, willingness, releasing judgment, asking for help when needed, and not allowing yourself to be invested in a certain outcome. We forgive for our own sake, not for the sake of someone else.

Power seduces. The power of righteousness, the power of righteous indignation, and the power of pure anger profoundly lure the injured ego. Yet, there is also the power to release one's grasp on their position, to surrender inward to what one feels inside, to forgive, and to love unconditionally. Herein lies a peace that cannot be broken, perturbed, or disturbed in any way, for it is pure, and it is the truth.

We cannot go back and change what happened. We must realize the destructive power of unresolved anger and resentment gnawing away inside us. Pain is the currency of transformation. We must be mindful of how we spend it. Hopefully, we can find forgiveness before things go too far and we become lost to ourselves forever. The act of forgiveness is an active process that allows us to transform pain into peace and live with ourselves again.

Elizabeth Kipp is an Addiction Recovery Coach (Recovery 2.0) Stress Management and Chronic Pain Specialist, Ancestral Clearing Practitioner, Bilateral EFT/ Tapping Practitioner, certified Kundalini Yoga Teacher (RYT/IKYTA), and author of *The Way Through Chronic Pain: Tools to Reclaim Your Healing Power.*" She holds a B.S. from the Univ. of Delaware. She pursued an M.S. in environmental studies at the University of Kansas with an emphasis on remote sensing, ecology, and environmental resource analysis. She has done basic and applied research and has authored and co-authored a number of peer-reviewed research papers.

Elizabeth Kipp is a long-time seeker of truths with a foot each in the spiritual and scientific worlds. Her life experiences and training enable her to bridge the gap between these two worlds.

In the months following the birth of her son in 1982, Elizabeth's burgeoning professional career was cut short by the emergence of a structural weakness in her low spine. She spent the next 31 years in and out of hospitals in pursuit of a way to stabilize her spine and find freedom from the persistent pain resulting from an old injury.

Her deep connection to the spiritual world supported her through multiple surgeries, decades of prescribed medications, and a long persistent search for modalities that would help her to heal. In 2013 Elizabeth entered a pain management program where she was able to free herself of the chronic pain cycle and find a way to live a life free of suffering.

Now in recovery, Elizabeth helps people to step into the power of their own healing. She has turned her attention as a patient advocate in service to the alarmingly high population of people who suffer from or are in recovery from chronic pain.

https://www.thewellnessuniverse.com/world-changers/elizabethkipp/

CHAPTER 25

STRESS AND THE HIGHLY SENSITIVE PERSON

MOVING BEYOND SURVIVING TO THRIVING

by Dr. Dolores Fazzino, DNP, RN, Nurse Practitioner, Medical Intuitive

MY STORY

We have all been there, at least I have. When you are born as a very sensitive child, you feel everything. My world was an endless exploration of my senses and emotions. I was a sponge absorbing all the emotion in my environment. I felt everything at a very deep level and felt that it was my job to fix it all. I thought this was normal, and not until I started exploring and healing my childhood issues, did I realize that this was anything but normal.

I would get emotional, feel situations very deeply, and take things on as my own, without knowing it. With no reference point or manual to decipher how to be on earth, I muddled through my childhood often misunderstood, not valued or appreciated, and very sad. I remember feeling "out of sorts" and not knowing how to "fit in". I wanted what any child would want, to be loved, seen, valued, and appreciated, particularly by their parents, and was not receiving this. It was a depressing time for me.

I grew up in the 1960s, a time where everything had to be perfect, you worried about what the neighbors thought about you, and it was all about appearances. Everything on the outside looked perfect, yet on the inside, it was another story.

It was not safe to let others see your feelings, so you did not do so because having feelings and emotions were considered a weakness. Feeling, oh, you just did not do that, particularly in my parent's home. Little did I know at that time this was not considered "normal" as well.

I was born into a world that does not feel their feelings or their emotions, and are judged, criticized, and even labeled as abnormal if you did. These emotions were stuffed, or ignored, or internalized, and even intellectualized, but rarely felt and experienced.

My parents just did not know what to do with me and my sensitivity. My mom's solution for me when I was feeling sad or uncomfortable was to ignore it. "It will go away," were her words. Unfortunately, this was not the case for me. As I tried to ignore what I was feeling, it would get even more intense. It was not going away.

My mother's coping mechanism for things she did not want to experience was to ignore it. I concluded my mother had a difficult childhood by putting the pieces together from stories shared from my mom's side of the family. It sounded to me as if my grandfather was an alcoholic. When I confronted my mother with this, she said that he was not because if there was no money, he would not drink, and if there was money, he would. That was not her definition of what an alcoholic was. However, my grandfather was a binge drinker and alcoholic. Now it was making complete sense as to why she acted the way she did. She suffered so much pain and anguish as a child; her coping mechanism was to ignore things and pretend that they were not there.

My mother finally admitted at age 60 that her father was an alcoholic. And now, her behavior and coping mechanisms were making complete sense to me. And her healing journey began.

My mom passed away at the age of 79 from stage four, pancreatic cancer. As a Medical Intuitive, I was not surprised since she spent a lifetime of ignoring her emotions, particularly the difficult ones. And since emotions are energy, when they are ignored, suppressed, internalized, and even intellectualized, the unexpressed energy from the emotion becomes trapped and stored in the body. It can create disease and/or illness. Once experienced, emotions become energetically neutral, with no lasting impact on a person's physical body. In my mom's case, I believe these emotions were trapped in her body and held in the pancreas. The late Louise Hay, the motivational author, claims the causes of symptoms for pancreatic cancer is "Not enjoying the sweetness of life."

I came into this world as an empath, intuitive, and highly sensitive person. I really did not know what all of this meant until I started my personal growth journey in my thirties. The triggering event for me was having a panic attack. I had been under so much stress as to please others, fix others, and do what I could to be perfect, that I pretty much snapped. I also could not figure out why my life was not working, while everyone else's was. I became severely depressed and knew that I needed help.

Interestingly, as I asked for help, the universe would provide opportunities for me to explore and learn more. I continued to follow their lead and still do to this day. Through my journey, I learned that what I was experiencing was a lack of strong, energetic boundaries. It made complete sense to me. There was nothing wrong with me, yet I was feeling the collective consciousness of the masses. The collective consciousness is a massive energetic form that contains all thoughts, beliefs, and emotions of individuals and the general population.

We can agree that everything is energy, as defined by the laws of quantum physics. Every experience that each of us has is an energetic one. Like radio waves and other invisible waves, our thoughts, beliefs, and emotions are energetically charged. Our responses continually contribute to the collective consciousness.

For example, if you are angry and hostile, that energy moves into the universe to the collective consciousness. The following visual will assist in better demonstrating this concept. Imagine your anger and hostility as a pebble, which represents you and these emotions. Next, imagine that this pebble is dropped into a still body of water, which will represent collective consciousness. Notice that as the pebble contacts the body of water, it creates a ripple in the still body of water, interacting with the body of water or collective consciousness. This is how each of us contributes our energy to the collective consciousness.

What makes it more challenging is being an Empath, Intuitive, and Highly Sensitive Person (HSP). This is so because you not only feel your responses, you also feel the responses of others in the collective consciousness. This is where energetic boundaries come into play and are necessary to decrease the stress one is receiving and experiencing.

Now, if you are an Empath, Intuitive, and HSP, you tend to feel things at a much deeper level than other people. People with this trait are the "energetic feelers" of humanity. They speak a different language and are fluent in feeling and reading energy. We are here on earth to help humanity return to the lost art of feeling and experiencing emotions.

A challenge for this group is personal boundaries, which tend to be enmeshed with other peoples' boundaries. Unconsciously, these people tend to take on other people's energy or collective consciousness and have difficulty discerning their stuff from someone else's. You may feel anxious, emotional, stressed out, or uncomfortable for no obvious reason.

As I progressed with my personal growth, I learned many tools and tricks to assist with creating energetic boundaries. As a healthcare provider for many decades, energetically, I took on others' emotional energy from collective consciousness each time I walked into the hospital setting. It was anxiety-producing and stressful. Having an arsenal of tools in my tool kit, was essential to my energetic health and wellbeing, and to decrease or eliminate the stress I was experiencing. Ninety-five percent of the time, what I was experiencing was not mine.

Have you ever felt that you were experiencing many different emotions in a short period, with not having any reason to be experiencing them? You are not alone. I have had this experience and thought I had gone mad or cray-cray, as I experienced *50 Shades of Emotion*. Let me remind you that you are not going CRAZY. You are taking on other people's emotions and tapping into collective consciousness.

I knew that I needed to find a way to make this all go away so that I could move beyond surviving to thriving.

I learned about the laws of the universe and free will as a human being. Since humans are here on earth with free will, nothing can interfere with you or your energy field unless you allow it. Interestingly, much of this unwanted invitation is on an unconscious level, meaning we are not aware this is happening. We are not aware that we are allowing it to happen.

"Nothing can come into your space energetically unless it is invited in."

– Universal Law

THE TOOL

I like to keep my tools as simple and as easy to use as possible. My philosophy is "less is more."

My go-to tool to discern what is mine versus someone else's energetically is one of the laws of the universe. The tool is very simple yet effective.

When you are feeling overwhelmed and stressed, do the following:

- Stop what you are doing
- Take a deep breath
- Say the following out loud or to yourself:
  If this is not my stuff, by the laws of the universe, remove yourself from my space immediately

Surprisingly, whatever uncomfortable feeling I might have been experiencing leaves, and I return to feeling at peace.

Everything flying around in collective consciousness these days: anger, rage, hate, fear, lack, etc.—all of which we are part of—can be a minefield. Even though the stress, anxiety, and other emotions, are invisible to the human eye, they are very much there energetically.

Being an Empath, Intuitive, and HSP myself, and working in the hospital setting for decades, I experienced collective consciousness firsthand. I would enter the hospital and feel completely drained, energetically spent, and fatigued. It was not until I realized how irritable I was, or sad, or angry, that I realized it was not me at all, but the environment I had entered.

When I started declaring to the universe that nothing was allowed to enter my energy field without my permission, I felt as if protective armor was surrounding my energy field and me. It allowed me to return to a neutral, peaceful, and serene place within myself. I felt empowered, safe, and secure. This was a complete game-changer for me. So I invite you to try it for yourself.

I continue to utilize this tool as needed in my life, somedays more than others. We are all on our paths. Just a reminder, we are all works in progress. Being aware is the first step to being able to make a shift or change.

Let's recap:

If you are unsure about what you are experiencing or feeling, declare to the universe, "If this is not my stuff, by the laws of the universe, remove yourself from my space immediately." and feel your world shift.

You've got this!

Dr. Dolores Fazzino, DNP, is a Nurse Practitioner, Medical Intuitive, and distinguished pioneer bridging the world of spirituality and wellness. With over 40 years of experience in the healthcare industry, she has assisted with over 13,500 surgical procedures. Gifted since she was a child with intuitive abilities, she is a master energy healer, medical intuitive, and visionary; she's always been on the cutting edge.

Dr. Fazzino believes healing is a multi-faceted process. By unraveling the energetic discord in her client's life, she assists her clients to heal in ways they never thought possible, integrating the emotional, mental, spiritual, and physical aspects of themselves to create lasting health and wellness. After witnessing the miraculous healing of her father's physical condition as a young adult, Dr. Fazzino has dedicated her life to assisting people to heal in ways they never thought possible.

She is an entrepreneur and creator of Spiritual Wellness for Life and Recovering Healthcare. Recognizing the many gaps in healthcare, Dr. Dolores takes us beyond the mind-body paradigm to include spirituality in wellness. This distinguished wellness practitioner offers customized programs and strategies to prepare patients through combining traditional medicine, energy healing, and intuitive counseling to assist clients in moving through life challenges and reconnecting with their inner self with grace and ease.

As the founder of Concierge Surgical Coaching®, she is the industry leader in preparing patients to heal faster and more completely from surgery, chronic illness, and other health and wellness concerns with her program model.

Additionally, she has authored several books, including *"54 Tips to Maneuver through the Healthcare System"* and *"Spiritual Wellness for Life."* Her next book, *"Healing In Ways You Never Thought Possible: A paradigm shift in health and wellness,"* will be available Spring 2021.

https://www.thewellnessuniverse.com/world-changers/doloresfazzino/

CLOSING CHAPTER

HIRING A WELLNESS PROFESSIONAL

TAKING YOUR HEALTH TO THE NEXT LEVEL

Our hope was to help you discover a new or better way to your best self and help you manage, relieve, and eliminate stress. All the experts here agree that empowering you by giving you tools to treat yourself at home is one of the keys to transformation and healing. When you take responsibility for self-awareness, self-care, self-healing, and self-development, you are much more apt to feel good and stay feeling that way. We've experienced clients who take self-treatment to heart getting better faster, staying healthier in the long run, and really enjoying their lives to the fullest.

We also know many people need skilled assistance and guidance to feel better. The clients we come across are in all stages of physical, mental, and emotional dis-ease or dysfunction. Some need a quick tool and home program, while others require intensive or prolonged care. We all agree that having a wellness guide on the journey is paramount to peak performance, whatever stage you're in.

When you have a wellness guide, coach, or healer in your corner, you'll reach your goals faster, but more importantly, you'll have someone invested in your progress and healing, and you won't be doing it alone. Remember, that guide has been where you are, and has healed the layers you're going through. He or she is able to hold a healing space for you to do that same work. Holding a healing space for you means they've practiced a conscious presence, an ability to ground and center themselves, and an ability to energetically enhance your healing process and have learned and practice modalities that work. That conscious presence is not something you find in all people. It's a practice that our wellness professionals, healers, coaches and skilled therapists have worked for years to master. They've adopted a lifestyle that includes these skills and tools, so they can help others. They are special, amazing people.

This final note is to encourage you to seek out a wellness guide if you feel like you're stuck, not making progress, feeling more hopeless than hopeful, or just can't consistently get your mindset to stay positive, open, or clear. We encourage you to explore different modalities and different wellness guides, coaches, and practitioners. Find someone you vibe with and hire them to help you get to where you want to go.

Try asking: What else is possible for my healing or transformation today? Just asking yourself that question should help you feel hopeful. Sit with that question without straining to hear an answer. Allow yourself to meditate on the possibility.

Another great question to sit with, and/or journal about: What if there's something you haven't learned yet that could change everything?

We sit around and think we've read it all, done it all, and learned it all, and we stay resigned to our current mediocre physical, mental, emotional status because we think there are no alternatives or options left. I've been exploring healing and the vast array of healing modalities for an entire lifetime, and I'm here to tell you I won't have time to get to all the possibilities.

Life is constantly changing and creates new circumstances and challenges. When we recognize and have an awareness around self-care, we can better and more quickly serve ourselves. Life itself creates an ongoing opportunity for us to better our experience with it.

There are people out there who will help you on this journey. There's a guide out there waiting to teach you something you didn't even know existed and expose you to another level of hope you didn't realize you could feel. This book outlines dozens of those approaches. Some traditional. Some alternative. Some you may have never heard of. Some you may have heard of but never tried. It's time to explore!

It's our job as authentic healers, practitioners, and guides to facilitate a process of healing in you, connect you with your inner healer and power, and super-boost that power inside you. And we're good at it. Try us!

Please go back to the chapters that drew you in, piqued your interest, or had you feeling a little excited. Look up the amazing author there and read a little bit more about them on www.TheWellnessUniverse.com You might even contact them to say thank you for their words, or set up a call with them to discuss what you learned. The authors I asked to be a part of this are cool like that; they want you to feel better, and they are open-hearted, skilled, and very aware and experienced wellness professionals. They thrive when you thrive. It's part of their mission, like it is mine, to help heal the world.

I hope you enjoyed this book. Even more than that, I hope you're getting into action with it, trying the exercises and tools, and getting some results! I'd love to hear how you're doing. Please share your story via www.TheWellnessUniverse.com the homepage will guide you where to submit your story and we would love to publish your true life experience. You will inspire others.

Lastly, I have a personal favor to ask. If you enjoyed this book and have a couple minutes to leave a review on Amazon, I'd greatly appreciate it. Your review helps others see our book, and it spreads the good vibes. Thank you!

Signing off now with a final wish for your best health. May you find what you need to thrive, mind, body, and soul and inspire others to be brave enough to give themselves the same.

Have a life to treasure,

Anna

A RAMPAGE
OF GRATITUDE

I feel deep appreciation and heart-felt gratitude to have such amazing, talented, beautiful people surrounding me and this book.

My thanks goes to God, my higher power, and everyone looking out over me from above. My mom included. Thank you. I know I am a big assignment and without you I could not do what I do.

Hugo Varela, my husband, my rock, my inspiration, my teacher, my love, my Prince. The most amazing human being I have ever met. Thank you for always believing in me and all your blessed support and love. I love you forever.

An incredibly special shout out to my Godparents and Best Friend Jeanne. Heartfelt gratitude to all my friends, family and mentors who have supported and encouraged me throughout my life. Every ounce of support I received from you personally allows me to create more success professionally and aids me to keep to my mission and serve those making the world a better place and create the space for well-being. Your love, compassion, and support are my foundation and springboard. At times you have seen something in me I did not see for myself. Without your love, support, and belief in me, I would not be where I am today. I am blessed and grateful.

My WU team. Without my team at The Wellness Universe, we would not be The Wellness Universe. Thank you, Jenny, Ashley, Vanessa, LE and Heather. Thank you to Shari Alyse who helped build WU with me through 2019.

Our Authors. Each of you have amazing gifts and share the mission to leave the world a better place. You touch countless lives with all you do as a resource for transformation, healing, and well-being. That takes a brave person. Thank you for being brave. Thank you for being a WU World-Changer.

Thank you to every member of The Wellness Universe community. You are what the world needs, now more than ever. Thank you for being a channel, guide, teacher, healer, coach, therapist, agent of change, way-shower, and support to all seeking to live their best lives.

Thank you to everyone who helped this book come into existence: Laura Di Franco and her team at Brave Healer Productions. Our designer, Dino Marino. Lynda Goldman whose original painting graces the cover.

And YOU. Our reader. You have taken a bold step and responsibility to help yourself. I applaud you for not only seeking your best life but taking the essential inspired action to create it. You have not only given yourself a gift, you have given a gift to all you love, and who love you. By creating a wonderful world for yourself, you create a wonderful world for those around you. My sincerest thanks.

SPECIAL THANKS TO OUR COVER ARTIST,
LYNDA GOLDMAN

 Lynda Goldman is an artist and author. Her Bachelor of Fine Arts degree took a long detour into writing 44 books with three major publishers, and coaching more than 25 health providers to becoming bestselling authors. She recently returned to her first love, playing with colors, shapes and lines in acrylics, inks and pastels. Join her on Instagram at lynda.goldman. Get her free report: 5 Steps to Decorate Your Home with Art You Love, Straight from an Artist, at: https://www.thewellnessuniverse.com/world-changers/lyndagoldman/

Share your personal story with The Wellness Universe. Support and inspire the world to experience a successful journey to well-being!

Have you tried the tools in this book? Have you worked with one of our wellness practitioners? Go to the link below and fill out the form. We will be publishing many of the stories submitted on our blog. https://blog. thewellnessuniverse.com/submit-your-story-to-the-wellness-universe/

Learn More About SoulTreat 2021 Wellness Retreat Now

Join us for SoulTreat, The Wellness Universe annual retreat. Come join us for workshops, talks, experiences, and events that will support your total well-being. Meet many of our authors in person! See details, schedule and more at www.WUSoulTreat.com

TheWellnessUniverse.com

Join The Wellness Universe as a practitioner of wellness (WU World-Changer) or as a seeker of well-being (WU Friend) today! https://www.thewellnessuniverse.com/join/

Check out what our members have to say!

Ilene Dillon, M.S.W.

I recommend The Wellness Universe

There IS no other organization doing what The Wellness Universe is doing; giving people who are working to help others and the planet to live in a state of ongoing wellness, to be successful in their jobs and in their reaching others to help them. I've been a Premium Plus Member for several years now, and value what Anna Pereira and her support people have created, and what they continue to infuse with creativity, opportunity, and support. A-mazing!

Deborah Roth

I recommend The Wellness Universe

As a WU "World Changer," I've been very impressed with the level of support they offer to us and the caliber of classes and blogs they make available to members. Everyone can benefit from being connected to the Wellness Universe, whether you're a wellness professional looking to expand your reach, or simply looking for an endless supply of wellness resources to empower and nurture your mind, body, heart and spirit.

Diane Boyko Achatz

I recommend The Wellness Universe

If you are in any way part of a Health and Wellness community, membership in The Wellness Universe will enhance both your personal and business life. With the most robust platform available, your success is guaranteed. when you are a member of The Wellness Universe.

Divine J9

I recommend The Wellness Universe

As an intuitive and empath, it's easy to know when intentions are pure. The Wellness Universe (WU) brings together heart-centered soulpreneurs with the purpose of truly making the world a better place, one soul at a time. Founder, Anna Pereira is incredibly supportive of the members, which helps to make WU feel like home.

Lisa Meisels

I recommend The Wellness Universe

The Wellness Universe is like home. It's a loving, supportive community to nurture your own growth and your business growth. I love this platform and would highly recommend it (and often do)!

ABOUT THE AUTHOR

Anna Pereira is the Founder of The Wellness Universe, and CEO of Soul Ventures, a woman-owned business, where her mission is to make the world a better place. She's an inspirational leader, mentor, and connector for business owners who are changing the world. As an author and creator of wellness events, projects, and programs, Anna is an expert at showcasing, promoting, and supporting the world's most talented wellness professionals.

Anna lives between Europe and her birthplace, New Jersey, USA with her husband, sports expert and investor, Hugo Varela. The couple have adopted pets (One dog and two cats), and care for two strays. Big Red, their African Gray, loves to speak English and Portuguese, and is the ruler of the house. Anna enjoys turning on the creative flow when time allows by painting, writing, and creating custom T-shirts and jewelry. Finding balance in nature or at the beach with friends is her joy. She's dedicated to serving her calling and leaving her legacy as a 'conduit for change' by bringing more health, happiness, and well-being to the world with a collaborative spirit and intentional action. Learn more about Anna and The Wellness Universe at TheWellnessUniverse.com.

"Anna Pereira is a visionary leader with incredible energy and passion for all things well-being. Her call to and enthusiasm for making the world a better place is contagious, and she inspires me to elevate my contribution to the world with her generosity of time, resources, and talent. Anna is a connector of people who share her enthusiasm for helping others be the best version of themselves. Her spark is igniting many of us to show up in ways we may not have done on our own, and that is making the world a better place."

–Laura Sharon, MA, ACC, CDTLF, CDWF

"I have worked with and alongside Anna for almost a year. She's a force of nature! My first experience was SoulTreat 2019 as a guest and participating health practitioner, and then several Wellness Universe events in 2020. She is incredibly focused, passionate, smart, and committed to excellence on all counts, including each and every time she interacts with someone, never leaving out a thank you. I'm always amazed at how she gets it all done, including that very important thank you and note of appreciation. Thanks Anna for all you do, how you do it, and for the profound difference you are making in the world."

–Laurie Levin, Certified Coach, Nutrition, Weight Loss,
Stress Reduction and Emotional Well-being.

"I've had the great privilege to be a part of Wellness Universe over the past year and most recently, to work closely with Anna Pereira, Founder, as both practitioner and participant in Wellness Universe's, SoulTreat Retreat.

Incredible doesn't convey my experience. Anna is a Dynamo!

Anna Pereira has a tremendous ability to adeptly motivate and inspire individuals to show-up and step-in to a collaboratively creative process that produces an outcome far greater than can be elicited by their individual parts. She generates the power of the whole, and it's transformative.

Anna leads as an example of true servant leadership, welcoming and walking alongside all members and guests of her events and groups with authenticity, an open heart, and in the spirit of collaboration. She asks each to show up in all of who we are, and to see and respond to a call to love and be loved; to inspire others and to be inspired; to say "Yes" to raising our consciousness and supporting those around us to also do the same. She "walks her talk" and requires the same of all of those who work with her.

I am deeply grateful for the time I was able to spend with Anna in one-on-one conversation after the close of SoulTreat. Although she needed some time to gather herself after this huge, 4-day event, she invited me in to have a conversation as two women, two leaders, and two hearts and souls with a shared desire to support others to rise up in greater love, compassion, authenticity, and power; to heal and renew, both in their own lives and in supporting others to do the same. As I shared with Anna, I understood we also align in knowing that as we give, we also receive. Working with Anna Pereira has been, and continues to be, both inspiring and a greater call to ramp up, to stand taller, and to step more confidently into my own work in the world as a holistic wellness leader and professional. I highly recommend Anna as a leader, mentor, and guide and encourage engagement with the Wellness Universe and SoulTreat Retreats to all wellness leaders, holistic practitioners, and to those who consciously seek to make a positive difference in their lives, the lives of others, and in the world."

–Jo Ann Wenner, Holistic Transformation Coach

Made in USA - Kendallville, IN
1200916_9781954047068
12.08.2020 1422